ARMING *your* CHILDREN *with the* GOSPEL

ARMING *your* CHILDREN *with the* GOSPEL

Creating Opportunities for Spiritual Experiences

R. WAYNE *and* LESLEE S. BOSS

DESERET
BOOK

SALT LAKE CITY, UTAH

Originally published in hardback under the title

Are My Children Going to Make It? Real Help
for Teaching the Gospel in the Home

First printing in hardbound 1991
First printing in paperbound 2003

Visit us at deseretbook.com

Library of Congress Cataloging-in-Publication Data

Boss, R. Wayne
    Arming Your Children with the Gospel: Creating Opportunities
for Spiritual Experiences / R. Wayne Boss, Leslee S. Boss.
        p.   cm.
    Includes bibliographical references and index.
    ISBN 0-87579-517-X (hardbound)
    ISBN 1-59038-214-5 (paperbound)
    1. Family – Religious life.   2. Christian education of children.
3. Mormon Church – Doctrines.   4. Church of Jesus Christ of Latter-
day Saints – Doctrines.   I. Boss, Leslee S., 1941–   II. Title.
BX8643.F3B67   1991
248.8'45—dc20
    [B]   91-15674

Printed in the United States of America   72076-7154
Publishers Printing, Salt Lake City, UT

10   9   8   7   6   5   4   3   2   1

This book is gratefully dedicated to our parents:

Russel Herbert and Elizabeth Thompson Boss
and
Lewis Kendall and Ione Anderson Swendsen

Contents

CONTENTS

Preface

President Spencer W. Kimball said, "The sad simple truth is that when we do not act preventively in the earlier years, we must later on act redemptively but with much less efficiency and fewer and more labored results!"[1] Effectively teaching children the gospel prevents problems and builds a foundation of gospel truths that will help them throughout the eternities.

The purpose of this book is to provide parents with ideas about ways to both simply and enjoyably teach their children the gospel. Each of the twenty-eight chapters begins with an introductory vignette or story based on a real-life experience, written in the first person, and designed to illustrate specific principles. The rest of the chapter contains counsel and examples from priesthood leaders, parents, and authorities in the field. Where appropriate, the names and some of the facts have been changed to insure anonymity.

This book began as a result of a priesthood assignment from our stake presidency. They asked us to write a training manual for the members of our stake on how to teach the gospel in the home. That initial manuscript, supplemented by interviews and additional research, provided the foundation for material contained herein.

In presenting the material in this book, we openly acknowledge our personal bias. If there are both enjoyable and miserable ways of doing something, and they produce equal results, we prefer to take the enjoyable routes. Since those whom we interviewed consistently reported how much they enjoyed teaching their children the gospel, we felt a need to share what we had learned.

Now a word of caution. This volume contains many ideas on teaching children. Some parents, therefore, may have unrealistic expectations of themselves and may become discouraged because they aren't doing everything we suggest. However, it would be impossible for a family to implement every idea contained in this book. Some ideas may be relevant to current circumstances; others may not. Other suggestions may need to be adapted to fit individual personalities and family relationships. It is helpful to remember that teaching children the gospel is a process, not an event. The needs of family members continuously change; thus, the need for flexibility in parenting to meet those changing needs.

We do not suggest that this book contains everything parents need to know about teaching children the gospel. One of the frustrating aspects of this project was the space limitations, which forced us to exclude relevant information about many important topics.

We also do not claim to be authorities on rearing children. We have our challenges, like other parents. We have made mistakes, and so have our children as they have exercised their agency. That is also true for everyone we know. Rearing children in light and truth is one of the most challenging assignments given to mankind. Indeed, we are continually humbled by the magnitude of that assignment, and we feel a need for all the help we can get.

In the course of doing our research, we interviewed people who we believed were effectively teaching their children the gospel. When we asked them what they did that helped their children understand gospel principles, all responded that they had a great deal to learn about the subject and hardly considered themselves to be experts. Most said that they wouldn't be able to tell how good a job they had done until their children were grown. One father said, "I suppose I won't know how effectively I have taught my children the gospel until I see how well my grandchildren turn out." There may be a great deal of truth in both statements.

In gathering our information, we are grateful for the contributions of many people. Specifically, we would like to thank

Kathleen Ammon, Robert and Jackie Ammon, John and Michelle Ammon, Jeff and Gayle Ammon, Stacia Ammon, David and Edna Allan, LeRoy and Larita Alldredge, Mark and Marie Alldredge, Bill and Lola Ruth Anderson, Mark and Marilyn Angus, David and Marlynn Angus, Stan and Helen Barrett, Leonard and Agnes Bishop, Chester and Aileen Boss, Lola Boss, Adam Dunford, Benjamin Dunford, Dan Dunford, Helen Dunford, Mitchell Dunford, Kelly and Wendy Ericson, John and Karen Foster, Kimberly Ann Foster, Jeffery Foster, Wade Foster, Adam Foster, Cheryl Gerdy, Richard L. Gunn, Revere and Blanche Hansen, Rashel Harrop, Cletus and Phyllis Hoer, Gordon and Claudia Holmstead, Kay and Mellie Holmstead, Lynn and Merica Hutchings, Dean and June Jessee, Donald and Katherine Jessee, James and Bonnie Johnson, Janice Johnson, Janece Johnson, Jared Johnson, Jason Karp, Dean and Laura Kunz, Jim and Nona Knighton, Jenna Langer, John and Caryol Linford, Matt Maxfield, Tom and Judy Maxfield, Mary Ann McConkie, Jerry and Janet McCoy, Dennis and Barbara Packard, Crystal Prentice, Angela Pulver, Melinda Pulver, Jonathan Rayback, Mike and Jeanne Rayback, Kathy Schlendorf Smith, Alex Spong, Stephanie Stearns, J. Delos and Trilva Thompson, Odell and Edna Mae Thompson, Merrill and Melba Wassom, Darren Wilhoit, Kathy Yorgason, Brenton and Margaret Yorgason, Jim and Elizabeth Ann Young, Brad Young, Greg Young, Kristy Young, Heather Young, David Young, and Eric Young. We also thank those who specifically requested that their names not be mentioned.

We wish to thank Blaine M. Yorgason for his encouragement and helpful suggestions at various stages of this project. Mark L. McConkie, Franklyn W. Dunford, and Don Norton also provided numerous helpful suggestions on various drafts of this manuscript. Margie Bonnes provided essential clerical support and made valuable contributions at every stage of the project.

We also appreciate the assistance and encouragement of Eleanor Knowles, Sheri Dew, Richard Tice, and the other members of the Deseret Book Company editorial staff.

In addition, we express our appreciation to our children—Scott Russel, Alan Dennis, Erin Camille, and David Spencer—for their patience, their love and support, and their insight on how we can more effectively teach them the gospel of Jesus Christ.

Most of all, we thank our parents, Russel and Beth Boss and Ken and Ione Swendsen, who taught us most of what we know about teaching the gospel in the home.

This is not an official church publication. Even though many people assisted in its preparation, we alone are responsible for the final product.

INTRODUCTION

1

Why Teach the Gospel in the Home?

The prophet's voice rang out clearly. "Make no mistake about it, you are a marked generation. . . . There has never been more expected of the faithful in such a short period of time than there is of us. . . . Never before on the face of the earth have the forces of evil and the forces of good been so well organized."

We sat spellbound. Over eight thousand five hundred seminary and institute students had gathered to hear President Ezra Taft Benson. I looked at my seven home-study seminary students and felt proud of the lives they were living. "While our generation will be comparable in wickedness to the days of Noah, when the Lord cleansed the earth by flood, there is a major difference this time: God has saved for the final inning some of His stronger and most valiant children, who will help bear off the kingdom triumphantly. . . . You are the generation that must be prepared to meet your God."[1]

Suddenly my thoughts turned to my own three children. If the wickedness of today was comparable to that of Noah's time, I had drastically underestimated the seriousness of the problems facing our family. A feeling of urgency came over me, and I wondered if my husband and I had sufficiently prepared our children to face the tribulations that lay ahead.

Why Teach the Gospel in the Home?

From the very beginning of time, the Lord commanded parents to teach the gospel to their children.[2] At the beginning of this dispensation, the Lord revealed the following:

3

Inasmuch as parents have children in Zion, or in any of her stakes which are organized, that teach them not to understand the doctrine of repentance, faith in Christ the Son of the living God, and of baptism and the gift of the Holy Ghost by the laying on of the hands, when eight years old, the sin be upon the heads of the parents. For this shall be a law unto the inhabitants of Zion, or in any of her stakes which are organized.

And their children shall be baptized for the remission of their sins when eight years old, and receive the laying on of the hands. And they shall also teach their children to pray, and to walk uprightly before the Lord. . . .

Now, I, the Lord, am not well pleased with the inhabitants of Zion, for there are idlers among them; and their children are also growing up in wickedness; they also seek not earnestly the riches of eternity, but their eyes are full of greediness. These things ought not to be, and must be done away from among them. (D&C 68:25–32.)

The Lord reinforced this sobering counsel eighteen months later by reminding the Saints, "I have commanded you to bring up your children in light and truth."(D&C 93:40.) He then promptly called Joseph Smith, Sidney Rigdon, and Frederick G. Williams, who constituted the First Presidency, and Newel K. Whitney, the first bishop of the Church, to repentance for not properly teaching their children the gospel. To Frederick G. Williams, for example, the Lord said, "You have not taught your children light and truth, according to the commandments; and that wicked one hath power, as yet, over you, and this is the cause of your affliction." (D&C 93:42.)

Thus, the responsibility for teaching children the gospel rests with their parents. Fortunately, as President Benson explained, we have adequate time to fulfill this obligation, since " 'power is not given unto Satan to tempt little children, until they begin to become accountable.' . . . The period of childhood and un-accountability was given to children so that 'great things may be required at the hand of their fathers.' " (See D&C 29:47–48.) President Benson then admonished parents, "Teach your children to understand principles of truth. . . . The Lord states that

Satan 'cometh and taketh away light and truth, through disobedience, from the children of men, and because of the tradition of their fathers' (D&C 93:39). The 'tradition of their fathers' refers, of course, to the bad examples and teachings of fathers."[3]

Elder Marion G. Romney provided additional insight on this point:

> Satan, our enemy, is making an all-out assault upon righteousness. His well-marshalled forces are legion. Our children and youth are the targets of his main thrust. They are everywhere subjected to wicked and vicious propaganda. Every place they turn, they are buffeted with evil, cunningly devised to deceive and to destroy every sacred thing and every righteous principle. . . . If our children are to be sufficiently strengthened to stand against this satanic onslaught, they must be taught and trained in the home, as the Lord has directed.[4]

There are a multitude of reasons why we need to teach the gospel in the home to our children. As Elder Romney clearly pointed out, children must understand the truth and have testimonies of the gospel so they can withstand the adversary. We also know that a knowledge of and faith in the saving principles of the gospel are necessary for exaltation. Children need to also gain a testimony of the divinity of Jesus Christ and his church.

Another compelling reason for us to teach our children the gospel is that by doing so, we are freed from the condemnation that would otherwise come. President Joseph F. Smith explained, "The parents in Zion will be held responsible for the acts of their children, not only until they become eight years old, but, perhaps, throughout all the lives of their children, provided they have neglected their duty to their children while they were under their care and guidance, and the parents were responsible for them."[5]

Great benefits will come to us and to our children when we teach the gospel of Jesus Christ in our homes. President David O. McKay said, "The Creator of the world ordained man and woman for the home, and He is seeing to it that they may search the whole world over but will never find the sweetest joys of life anywhere but in the home."[6] By teaching the gospel in the home, Latter-day Saint parents can say, as did John of old, that "I have no greater joy than to hear that my children walk in truth.' (3 Jn 1:4.) That joy can be achieved only by obeying the commandments and keeping our covenants and obligations.

2

The Power
of the Family

"But Mom," my twelve-year-old son pleaded, "they'll make fun of me because of the things I can't do and because of how I am!"

"No one will make fun of you," I replied. "I won't let that happen. I promise you that we'll only have feelings of love for you."

"I don't want to do it!"

"That's fine. You don't have to. But rather than give me an answer now, why don't you think about it overnight and then let me know what you decide?"

John, the second youngest of our children, had not adjusted well to the seventh grade. He had no friends, strongly disliked school, and got straight Fs on his first-quarter report card. Predictably, his self-esteem had dropped to almost zero. When I suggested that we have a family fast day in his behalf, everyone agreed except John. He didn't want his brothers and sisters to laugh at him. Fortunately, he believed what I told him, and the next day he agreed to a family fast day.

At 5:00 P.M. on the day of the fast, we met in the living room, dressed in our Sunday clothes. I related a true-life experience about a family who had faced serious difficulties and, through fasting and prayer, received great blessings from the Lord. My husband and I each bore testimony that Heavenly Father would also help us as a family if we worked together. We told the children that anyone who wanted to could offer a prayer, but we didn't want them to feel pressured to do so.

7

We then knelt together, and Rick, our youngest, said he wanted to go first. That little boy offered one of the sweetest prayers I have ever heard. All the others in turn offered wonderful prayers in behalf of John.

At first, John was embarrassed. I had my arm around him, and I could feel how tense he was. Whenever others mentioned his name, he giggled nervously. However, by the time that Glen, the third person to pray, offered a prayer, John had become much more serious and comfortable. When his turn came, he offered a sincere and touching prayer pleading with the Lord for help.

My husband then gave John a blessing. When he finished, John hugged his dad; the two of them stood for several minutes, arms around each other, crying. Our son then hugged and kissed every family member. The Spirit was as strong as I have ever felt it.

The details of the later counseling sessions, the meetings with teachers, the homework assignments, and the hours spent trying to help our son feel good about himself are all important, but what is most important is the strength that experience brought into our family. We now realize that our family can experience great spiritual power when we combine our faith and work together in unity, love, and harmony.

The Power of the Family

Regarding the importance of the family, President Joseph Fielding Smith gave us this instruction: *"The family is the most important organization in time or in eternity. . . .* Love each other with all your hearts. Keep the moral law and live the gospel. Bring up your children in light and truth; teach them the saving truths of the gospel; and make your home a heaven on earth, a place where the Spirit of the Lord may dwell and where righteousness may be enthroned in the heart of each member."[1]

Parents who work to make their homes a heaven on earth are creating families with unlimited spiritual potential. Indeed, few forces can equal the power of righteous, united families. For this reason alone, we can understand why Satan wants to destroy families.

Of all the tools at Satan's disposal, few more potently destroy

THE POWER OF THE FAMILY

family unity and love than criticism, which is a deadly poison that decreases self-esteem, damages family relationships, and fosters resentment, antagonism, and contention. Criticism is also depressing and discouraging. Our children may readily accept our critical comments as facts and actually begin to see themselves as worthless and incapable of succeeding. They may also become defensive and unmotivated, and eventually they stop listening to us. If we want healthy relationships with our children, based on mutual trust and communication, we need to stay as far from criticism as possible. Indeed, we can learn much from watching how well computers help children to learn. *Computers never criticize!* For good reason, then, the Lord commanded us to "cease to find fault one with another." (D&C 88:124.)

Of course, there are times when children need to be corrected. In fact, children require constant teaching and correction. But the tone and intent of that teaching need to be positive rather than critical or destructive. There is a big difference between criticizing children in ways that destroy self-esteem and drawing attention to their negative behaviors.

On the other hand, few things contribute to family unity and strength quite so much as concentrating on our children's positive behaviors. In connection with this, President David O. McKay said, "I do not know of anything that will contribute more to unity . . . than for [family] members to see the good . . . and to speak well of each other."[2] A father recounted the following example:

> It almost seemed as if our kids had a contest to see who could tell the worst story, in terms of complaining about all the terrible things that happened to them each day. That negative attitude spilled over into everything they did, including their interaction with family members. It was awful.
>
> Six months ago we decided to concentrate on the positive things. Since the dinner table was the only place we were all together as a family, we started there. Each evening as we ate, I asked, "What is the best thing that happened to you today?" At first I was met with dead silence. None of my four children could think of a single positive thing that had happened to them. They had concentrated so much on

9

the negative that they were oblivious to the positive. However, over the next few weeks that slowly changed, until now they regularly take the initiative and delight in sharing with us their success experiences. If I forget to ask the question, they often raise it. Concentrating on the positive has helped make a major transformation in our home.

In order to have unity in our homes, family members need to feel valued, accepted, and appreciated. That can't happen when children constantly fight and put one another down. Rude and abrasive behavior rapidly destroys family unity. Therefore, we need to teach our children from infancy that discourteous and disrespectful outbursts will not be tolerated.

Fortunately, we can do a great deal to build cohesiveness and unity in our homes. To do so, however, we must be willing to make harmonious family life a high priority. A mother of four teenagers described how they addressed the issue of building self-esteem in their family:

> To establish a positive environment in our home, we agreed to the following rule: We don't say or do anything that undermines the self-esteem of another family member. That means we don't belittle, demean, or make fun of each other. We don't call each other names, and we don't put each other down. We take this rule very seriously because it's a matter of survival for us. Our kids get knocked around enough on the outside without having that kind of nonsense in their own family.
>
> Some parents maintain that "fighting like cats and dogs" is normal for children. I disagree, and we don't permit our children to do it. The Lord commanded us to not let our children "fight and quarrel one with another." Rather, "teach them to love one another, and to serve one another." [Mosiah 4:14–15.] When they feel loved, they learn to trust others, to serve others, and to accept others for who they are. Feeling truly loved and valued will help them blossom and achieve their potential. Children don't flourish in an environment where they are always having to watch their flank.

Building self-esteem in children is essential for them to have emotionally healthy and productive lives; and nobody can help them develop self-esteem better than we can. A father noted:

> As far as I'm concerned, a high level of self-esteem is one of the most important gifts I can give my children. It is a gift from me that will last a lifetime. When children have self-esteem, they *feel* lovable and *feel* worthwhile. Therefore, it isn't enough just to love them. My job is to help them *feel* loved, and I can't start that process early enough. The more important I can help them feel, the better off they will be.
>
> Some parents believe that their kids will grow up to be conceited if they tell them they're wonderful. That's hogwash! If kids don't feel important in their own home, they will have a tough time filling that void in school or other settings. I consistently tell my own children how wonderful they are, and I carefully reinforce those observations by identifying specific things they do well. That builds self-confidence. When they have confidence, they are less fearful of challenges. When they feel important, they are also more inclined to behave like somebody of value, which means that they are more inclined to live gospel standards.

One of the reasons significant changes take place in the lives of new converts to the Church is that they have been taught the gospel and have come to understand who they *really* are. They know they are sons and daughters of God; and that makes loving the Lord easier. The same is true for children, as the following example illustrates:

> One night, as I was putting my three-year-old daughter to bed, I asked, "Alice, what do you think Jesus would say if he walked into your bedroom right now?"
>
> "Daddy, he'd say, 'Who is that beautiful little girl in the pretty pink pajamas?' Then he'd come over here and hold me and kiss me good night." That little girl clearly understood her relationship with her Father in Heaven and his Son. Little wonder, then, that she has grown up wanting to keep the commandments.

As much as ninety percent of our behavior is designed to

make us feel important. Understandably then, we are drawn like a magnet to people who help us feel good about ourselves. We want to be around them. We want to work for them. We want to live with them. We also trust them and believe what they tell us. It is not surprising, then, that teaching the gospel to our children is much easier when it is accompanied by praise, listening, understanding, acceptance, respect, and admiration — all of which are ways of letting them know how valuable they are. Such conditions foster family unity and cohesiveness.

As the Lord knelt in the upper room before he went to Gethsemane, he offered the great intercessory prayer in which he prayed for unity, "That they may be one, even as we are one." (John 17:22.) This unity can be brought about in several ways. For example, doing things together as a family binds family members together. As a father of three explained, "Something happens to the family when everyone participates, particularly if one of the children is performing. When the whole family takes the time to go to a piano recital, a baseball game, or a school activity, they have clearly made a statement about the child's importance. When the entire family does things together, they draw upon the powers of heaven as they can in no other way."

The Savior said, "Be one; and if ye are not one ye are not mine." (D&C 38:27.) This has implications for how we work together as a family and how much everyone is involved. A father of four teenagers described the impact of including all the family members in problem-solving meetings.

We have continuously involved all our family in problem-solving meetings. When the children were younger, we were tempted to withhold information from them because of their inability to understand what was going on. However, we wisely chose not to do that. As a result, some of our most spiritual family experiences have happened when one of us had a problem.

By including every family member in the serious matters affecting us, we have become stronger as a family. The adversity we feel binds us together, and we have spiritual experiences that we could have in no other way. We feel loved and supported by each other. We are more unified, and the process provides each of us the opportunity to experience the application of the gospel. We have memories of these experiences that are sweet.

Working together also provides a training ground for our children and gives my wife and me an opportunity to see how they respond when things become difficult. Our children have gained skills in dealing with difficulties and in resolving problems. We have come to better understand how much our Heavenly Father wants to help us with our problems. In the process, our children have learned how to call upon the powers of heaven to bless them in their lives.

President David O. McKay said, "The poorest shack in which love prevails over a united family is of greater value to God and future humanity than any other riches. In such a home God can work miracles and will work miracles."[3] A mother of five described the fulfillment of that promise:

> Several years ago, our only daughter was diagnosed with an incurable disease. We called a family council, and everyone attended, including our three- and five-year-old sons. Because of their tender ages, we weren't sure if they could understand, but we were surprised at their sensitivity. We decided during that meeting to hold a family fast in our daughter's behalf.
>
> At the conclusion of our fast, we knelt together as a family, and each of us offered a fervent prayer for her. Our little boys offered sweet, sincere prayers for their sister — they prayed so hard that she would be all right. The spirit was strong in our home.
>
> After we finished, my husband called another Melchizedek Priesthood holder, and they administered to our daughter. She was instantly healed of her affliction. In the process, we learned more about the power of the combined faith of family members and the Lord's statement, "Suffer little children, and forbid them not, to come unto me: for of such is the kingdom of heaven." (Matt. 19:14.)

Miracles, of course, come in countless ways, but the important thing to remember is to create the unity and love in the family that allow the Lord to operate in our homes. Under these conditions, blessings will be poured out upon family members. As the Lord declared, "Eye hath not seen, nor ear heard, neither have entered into the heart of man, the things which God hath prepared for them that love him." (1 Cor. 2:9.)

CREATING
THE CLIMATE
FOR TEACHING
THE GOSPEL
IN THE HOME

3

Creating Opportunities
for Spiritual Experiences

I admired her courage. As a single parent with four children, she was doing her best to care for her family, hold down a part-time job, and keep up on the requirements of two college classes. Given the strain on her finances, the chances of her family having a Thanksgiving dinner two days later appeared remote.

After she left my office, I called my wife, told her of the woman's plight, and suggested that we do what we could to help. My wife responded enthusiastically, and that evening six bags of groceries sat on our kitchen table.

Steve, my oldest son, who was eight at the time, went with me to deliver the foodstuffs. We carefully placed them on the doorstep and then quickly drove away to avoid being seen. After returning home, Steve called the woman and, without identifying himself, suggested that she open the front door. We then drove past their house to make certain that the groceries had been taken inside.

On the way home, I noticed tears running down Steve's cheeks. "Is anything the matter?" I asked.

"Dad, is this what it's like to feel the Holy Ghost?"

"Yes, Son, this is exactly what it feels like."

"I've always wondered what it was like to feel the Holy Ghost. I won't forget this feeling as long as I live." I silently thanked my Father in Heaven for the witness he had given my son of the importance of serving others.

Can Spiritual Experiences Be Created?

Spiritual experiences cannot be created. However, we can create a climate in which spiritual experiences can occur. In fact, the programs and meetings of the Church are designed to create such opportunities.

The secret to having spiritual experiences is to have the companionship of the Holy Ghost, "which is the gift of God unto all those who *diligently seek him.*" (1 Ne. 10:17; italics added.) Implicit in that statement is the message that if we are to have the companionship of the Holy Ghost, we must diligently seek the Spirit. As a father of nine recently explained,

> If you are sitting around, waiting for spiritual experiences to happen to your children by accident, you're wasting your time. They won't. Spiritual experiences are never accidental. Our business is to create a climate in which they can take place. That's why in our meetings we sing hymns, preach, pray, and bear testimony. That's also why we have family home evening and family prayer and why we go to the Lord in our private closets. These activities are designed to bring the Holy Spirit into our lives.

> A lot of people complain because they never have spiritual experiences, but they don't do anything to foster them. We have to work for spiritual experiences. Joseph Smith prayed that his faith would be increased,[1] and he taught that spiritual power can be obtained by fasting and prayer.[2] Keep in mind that Joseph said these things *after* he experienced the First Vision, *after* he saw Christ and the prophets in the Kirtland Temple, and *after* he received the revelation describing the three degrees of glory. Even with those experiences, he fasted and prayed that his faith would be strengthened. If fasting and prayer helped Joseph increase his faith, it will certainly help me increase mine.

If we want blessings from God, we must prepare ourselves to receive them. If we want spiritual experiences, we must diligently try to keep the laws upon which those blessings are predicated. We must plan for them, and we must work hard to earn the right to receive them. In short, we must do everything within our power to gain the blessings we seek.

18

Why is it that some people have more spiritual experiences than others? A grandfather of twenty-seven gave the following explanation:

First, they seek spiritual experiences. They want them badly, and they ask the Lord for them. Throughout the scriptures, the Lord frequently tells us, "Ask and ye shall receive." One of the reasons people don't have more spiritual experiences is because they don't bother to ask for them.

Second, they fully expect to have spiritual experiences. They take the Lord at his word when he said, "Whatsoever things ye shall ask the Father in my name shall be given unto you." [3 Ne. 27:28.] When they pray, they fully expect that their prayers will be answered.

Third, they create an environment in which spiritual experiences occur. That is done by obeying the commandments. They also participate in Church programs, attend their meetings, study the scriptures, kneel in prayer, and do everything in their power to "live by every word that proceedeth forth from the mouth of God." [D&C 84:44.]

Fourth, they are personally worthy to receive the blessing they seek. They follow the Lord's direction and prepare themselves "by doing the things which [he has] commanded [them] and required of [them]." [D&C 78:7.] They must not only be good, but also do good.

Finally, they go to those places where the Holy Ghost is present. That is one of the reasons the Lord has commanded us to meet together often in church meetings—so he can bless us with his Spirit. That is one of the reasons why the temple is called the House of the Lord—because it is the best environment on the earth for having spiritual experiences. Temples are the purest places on earth: they have been dedicated and set apart as places where the Lord will manifest himself to his people. [See D&C 109:5.]

However, temples and other church buildings are not the only places where the Holy Ghost is present. One of the most sacred places on earth can be the home, and those who enter righteous homes feel the influence of the Spirit. As one young man explained:

19

One of the reasons I love to bring my friends to our home is to give them a chance to feel the Spirit that we have there. Almost without exception, everyone who comes through the front door stops, looks around, and says, "Wow. This is really neat." They don't know what they are feeling, but they like it. After the senior prom, my date and I, along with two other couples, came back to our home to spend the rest of the evening. I still remember my girlfriend sitting in the rocking chair in our living room and saying, "I really feel comfortable in your house. There is something here that I really like." Little did she know that what she was feeling was the Holy Ghost.

Rearing children is a spiritual process, and children gain testimonies by having spiritual experiences. Under such conditions, the Holy Ghost bears witness to them that Jesus is the Christ, that Joseph Smith is a prophet, and that the restored gospel is true. As parents, we ought not leave these experiences to accident. Fortunately, opportunities can be created for children to feel the influence of the Holy Ghost. The remaining chapters of this section provide ideas about how parents can create conditions under which sacred experiences can take place.

4

Teaching Children
to Listen to the Spirit

As I walked out of my Sunday School class, I was so choked up I could hardly talk. It had been one of the spiritual highlights of my entire senior year. I looked at Mike, smiled, and said, "Wow. That was great!"

"I don't believe a thing he said," Mike retorted.

"What?" I couldn't believe what I was hearing.

"He made up every one of those stories. There is no way they could have happened to him. Things like that don't happen to people today. They happened in the Bible and in the Book of Mormon. They might even happen to some of the General Authorities today. Maybe. But they don't happen to people here in our ward, and they certainly didn't happen to him."

By this time the other kids in our Sunday School class had joined us in the hall. "How do you know those things didn't happen to him?" I asked.

"I just know," Mike said flatly. "I've never had those kinds of experiences. Neither has anybody that I know of. If he is really that close to God, why isn't he a General Authority? He isn't even a bishop. He's only a Sunday School teacher. I think he stole those experiences from somebody else and said they were his. The Lord has never given me those kinds of experiences, and he isn't going to give them to anyone else, either."

"I can't believe what I'm hearing. You sound just like Laman and Lemuel. I felt the Holy Ghost in that class. I know how I felt. You can't tell me that what he said isn't true. I felt it."

21

"He was just playing on your emotions," Mike argued. "I got sucked into it for the first part of class, but then I realized what he was doing."

"You didn't get sucked into anything. That was the Holy Ghost you felt."

"Nonsense. That was just your emotions. You've been deceived. That guy knows how to work a group."

I was stunned. I had just listened to one of the best Sunday School lessons I had ever heard in my life, and my friend had no idea that what he was feeling was the Holy Ghost.

Teaching Children to Listen to the Spirit

A testimony of the gospel of Jesus Christ comes when the Holy Ghost bears witness to us that the gospel is true. Since that witness is a private experience, we cannot safely assume that our children will recognize that witness when it happens. So we can help them immeasurably by teaching what receiving revelation and having spiritual experiences feel like. A bishop described the insight he gained about how to better serve the youth in his ward:

> Recently I accompanied twenty-eight young people from our ward to the temple to do baptismal work for the dead. Before the baptisms began, the temple president spoke to us, and I was particularly interested in a comment he made. He said, "If you are worthy to come into the temple, you are worthy to go to the celestial kingdom. That means that you are worthy to enter the presence of God, and you are entitled to all of the spiritual gifts that God has in store for those who love and serve him."
>
> I thought to myself, "If that's true, then why aren't our young people having more spiritual experiences? They've been given the gift of the Holy Ghost. They have the right to the constant companionship of the Spirit. They're certainly worthy of that great blessing." Yet several of our youth had told me in interviews that they had never had any spiritual experiences. I found that hard to believe, given the kind of lives they were leading. They had every right to receive revelation and to have their prayers answered.

22

The Spirit then bore witness to me that most of them had received *numerous* revelations and had been blessed with many spiritual experiences. However, they didn't know what having a witness from the Holy Ghost felt like, so they had nothing with which to compare those experiences.

Perhaps the main reason children are unable to recognize the companionship of the Holy Ghost is that their parents haven't taught them what to expect. Sometimes that happens because parents don't have testimonies themselves, and teaching something you don't know is tough. Other parents may have spiritual experiences, but, like their children, they are unable to recognize them. As Dallin H. Oaks explained,

> I know from experience that some seasoned members of the Church do not know when they are receiving a witness of the Spirit. . . .
>
> Perhaps lifelong members of the Church don't recognize the testimony of the Spirit because they have had it so often they take it for granted. Perhaps they are looking for something startling and different. . . .
>
> I have heard adult members of the Church claim they do not have a testimony because they have never experienced a "burning in the bosom." (D&C 9:8.)
>
> If I thought this scriptural "burning" only referred to caloric heat, I would have to say that I have never had a burning in the bosom either. . . . In this usage, it does not seem to refer to heat but rather to an intensity of feeling.
>
> For me, the witness of the Holy Ghost is an intense feeling of serenity or well-being.[1]

Other parents do not teach their children what receiving a witness from the Holy Ghost feels like because they have the mistaken notion that young people are incapable of understanding things of the Spirit. Consider, for example, the following experience:

> Recently a friend described the difficulty she was having with her daughter. The fifteen-year-old girl was in love with a boy and was furious that she couldn't date until she turned

23

sixteen. Her anger had begun to spill over into other areas, and she had started questioning some of the basic principles of the gospel.

After my friend finished her story, I said, "I'm sure that your daughter will continue to flounder with these issues until she goes to the Lord and seeks his guidance. The Holy Ghost will testify to her the answers to her questions."

The mother replied, "You don't understand. My daughter is only fifteen. She's too young and immature to understand the promptings of the Spirit."

Shocked, I said, "Throughout history, young people have responded to the Spirit's promptings. The Prophet Joseph Smith was only fourteen when God and Jesus Christ appeared to him. Mormon was your daughter's age when the Savior appeared to him. Many young people are converted to the Church during their teens. Your daughter was given the gift of the Holy Ghost when she was eight, and that means that she has the right to the constant companionship of the Spirit."

"You're right. I hadn't thought of that."

"One crucial element in gospel training is knowing how to create opportunities for our children to have spiritual experiences and then help them understand what they felt."

"Are you sure you can do that? I thought spiritual experiences just came to people."

"If you just wait for them to come along, nothing will happen. But you can create opportunities for spiritual experiences, and the Lord will support you and bless you for your efforts. There are many things you can do as a mother to help your daughter become more spiritual, as long as you don't underestimate her capacity to understand things of the Spirit."

Since a spiritual witness from the Holy Ghost is a private matter, there is no guarantee that children will recognize the Spirit when it comes. Spiritual growth accompanies experience. It is a gradual process and comes line upon line, precept upon precept. Just as intellectual growth comes with hard work and sacrifice, so does spirituality. As the Holy Ghost bears witness to us over and over again that gospel principles are true, our faith increases and our knowledge of gospel principles becomes certain. The easiest way to help children learn these valuable lessons is to place them in situations where the Spirit of the Lord is present and then point out to them what they have experienced. Under those circumstances, children can be taught what it *feels* like to have the Spirit affect them. Note, for example, the insight that was gained by an Aaronic Priesthood holder:

> One of the great learning experiences of my life occurred at our dinner table one fast Sunday when I was a junior in high school. While discussing the testimony meeting we had attended earlier that day, I told my father that it was one of the best meetings I had ever attended.
>
> "Why do you say that?" he asked.
>
> "I don't know for sure. I liked what people said. But the thing I liked best was the way I felt."
>
> "How did you feel?"
>
> After thinking about it, I said, "It's hard to explain. I felt warm inside. Sometimes I kind of tingled. Sometimes I felt something like the chills, except I wasn't cold. I noticed it most when Brother Forsberg bore his testimony."
>
> Dad then said, "What you felt today was the Holy Ghost. I felt it very strongly myself. It affects people differently. Now you know for sure what it feels like to have the Holy Ghost bear witness to you that a gospel principle is true. That's what it feels like to have the companionship of the Holy Ghost. Never forget those feelings. Satan can't duplicate them. When you feel that way, you can feel confident that you have the companionship of the Holy Ghost."
>
> I was amazed. So that's how it felt. I had always wondered what feeling the Spirit of the Lord was like, but I had never been able to identify it. Therefore, I had claimed that I had never had any spiritual experiences.
>
> Once I knew what to expect, I was able to recognize those feelings in the future. I also realized that I had been blessed with many spiritual experiences throughout my life—I just didn't know what had caused those feelings.

What kind of feelings, then, can we help our children identify as the effect of the Holy Ghost? As with most other gospel principles, the scriptures clearly and powerfully tell us. The Topical Guide in the LDS edition of the Bible, for instance, refers to so many feelings from and experiences with the Spirit or Holy Ghost that listing them all is almost impossible. Following are just a handful of examples:

Paul makes a list of many of the "fruits" of the Spirit, specifying "love, joy, peace, longsuffering, gentleness, goodness, faith, meekness, temperance." (Gal. 5:22–23.) The Comforter may fill us "with hope and perfect love." (Moro. 8:26.) Our hearts may swell with joy because of the Spirit. We may experience peace.[2]

The Spirit may also help us suddenly remember things when we need them. He may comfort us.[3] He may help us recognize truth, especially concerning God the Father and Jesus Christ.[4] He may make us clean and pure.[5] He may lead us to and strengthen our desire to walk uprightly and do justly.[6] He may even give us prophecies, dreams, and visions.[7] So the question for our children is not so much "When will I experience the Holy Ghost?" but rather "How can I recognize the many times the Holy Ghost has affected me?"

Family testimony meetings also provide unique opportunities for spiritual experiences and, at the same time, provide the freedom to talk instructively about what family members have felt. A young father recalled the following:

> The experience I remember most when I was little was a testimony meeting we held as a family. Dad, Mom, and we five kids each bore our testimonies and said how much we loved each other. I resisted participating, because I did not know that the gospel was true. So Dad wisely asked me to bear testimony to what I knew was true. I talked about God answering prayers and about people being healed. When I said, "I know that the gospel is true," I felt the Holy Ghost bear witness to me that my words were true. I will never forget how I felt when that happened. Dad pointed out that those feelings were what it's like to receive a witness from the Holy Ghost.
>
> I have since learned the genius of that experience, and I now hold regular testimony meetings with my own family.

We strengthen each other with our testimonies and expressions of love for one another. These meetings also provide
an opportunity for the Holy Ghost to bear witness to our
children that the words they themselves say are true and
to feel the Holy Ghost in an environment where we can
explain to them what is happening.

Developing spirituality is an individual responsibility. We
can help our children achieve it, but the ultimate responsibility
falls on them. No one can force spirituality on them. But they
do need to be taught how to recognize that the Holy Ghost is
bearing witness to them of the truthfulness of the gospel. Their
lives will be much richer and their testimonies much firmer if
we do.

5

The Power of Example

I felt someone squeeze my arm. When I opened my eyes, I saw my father kneeling beside me as I lay in my sleeping bag on the kitchen floor by the telephone. Even though I was fourteen and almost as big as he was, Dad took me in his arms, as he had so many times when I was little, and said eight words that I will never forget: "Son, your mother died about twenty minutes ago."

I clearly recall the events of the next three days: selecting the casket, planning the funeral, viewing Mother's body in the living room of Aunt Agnes and Uncle Leonard's home, attending the funeral, dedicating the grave, and riding the lonely, seventy miles home with my father and my three younger sisters, ages ten, six, and three.

I also remember the difficult days, weeks, and months that followed. During that time, Dad's unwavering faith in God seemed almost miraculous. I watched him closely as he sought the Lord in prayer and pled for strength to deal with his grief and for wisdom to help meet the needs of his heartbroken children. Not once did I sense any bitterness, anger, or resentment. He loved the Lord and put his trust in him. He knew the Lord loved him and his children, and he sought the comfort and companionship of the Spirit that Christ has promised to those who mourn. He frequently spoke of the blessings we had as a family and expressed his gratitude to the Lord for helping us face our challenges and trials.

The faith I saw my father exercise after Mother's death has been a great source of strength to me as I have experienced the trials, vicissitudes, and tribulations of mortality. His example had more influence on my life than all the discussions we had about the principles of the gospel.

The Power of Parental Example

Teaching by example is basic to teaching our children, since we cannot teach with power a principle we do not live. As President Brigham Young explained, "If each and every one of us who are parents will reflect upon the responsibilities devolving upon us, we shall come to the conclusion that we should never permit ourselves to do anything that we are not willing to see our children do. We should set them an example that we wish them to imitate."[1]

Thus, the best way to teach children honesty is to be honest ourselves. We most effectively teach children to love by loving them. We teach compassion by being compassionate. What they see and how they feel will have a far greater impact on their values and attitudes than the words they hear. Great lessons are learned from the silent sermons we preach through the way we live. For example, consider how one woman learned the importance of prayer:

> I don't recall my folks ever talking to me about prayer, though I'm sure they must have. I don't even remember any family home evening lessons on it. Prayer was just something that happened in our home, and we took it so much for granted that I assumed everybody did it. As a result, I learned to pray from listening to my parents pray. Every morning and evening without fail, and sometimes in between, we knelt around the kitchen table in family prayer. Guests were always invited to join us. There was never the slightest indication of any embarrassment about kneeling before the Lord. It seemed just as natural as the meal that followed.

Parents are the most effective examples children will have. As they see us live the principles of the gospel, they understand much more clearly the importance of the gospel themselves.

They are then able to translate those principles into productive behavior. As a mother of three said,

> People have often asked why I'm so kind and considerate. If I do have those traits, the main reason is that I never heard my mother say anything unkind about anybody. On many occasions I heard people tell her things about others that I knew she already knew, because I had overheard other conversations. However, she never divulged confidences, and she never gossiped. As I was growing up, I thought that was a classy way to act, and I prided myself on doing the same. That decision saved me a lot of grief, because nobody ever accused me of talking behind their backs or saying hurtful things about anybody. People knew I would keep my mouth shut, and so they trusted me with things that they'd tell no one else.

When children see our behaviors as consistent with the principles we teach, they trust us and tend to adopt our values. As a stake president reported,

> The main reason I love the scriptures is because my dad loved them. Throughout his life, I was continuously impressed with his faithfulness in studying the scriptures. He read them constantly. On many occasions, while reading, he would say, "Son, I didn't know this," and then proceed to tell me about something "new" he'd discovered while reading the Book of Mormon for the "nth" time. Since I love my father, it is only natural that I love the things he loves. I want to be like him.

Very few parental behaviors miss the watchful eyes of children; they can tell when we practice what we preach. As they observe our obedience, they better understand the need for obedience in their own lives. For example, a mother of two learned about the importance of tithing in the following way:

> I learned to pay tithing by watching my parents. Every fast Sunday the family gathered around the kitchen table with the tithing envelopes. We had our banks. Mom and Dad had their checkbook. We each determined the amount of money we had earned that month, filled out the tithing

receipts, put our tithing in the envelopes, and sealed them up. I remember how important I felt when I did that. My folks usually recounted the blessings the Lord had given us and told us what an honor it was to give him something in return. Occasionally they talked about how the tithing money was used. As a result, there was never a time when I didn't feel good about paying tithing.

We also teach our children powerful lessons by the way we treat others, particularly those who "revile [us] and persecute, and . . . say all manner of evil against [us] falsely." (3 Ne. 12:11.) As one young man explained,

> Eight years ago, before my folks were divorced, Dad sat down with each of us individually and again as a group and told us that we would never hear him say anything negative about our mother. He wanted us to have a close relationship with her, and he would do everything he could to see that we felt that way.
>
> Dad kept his promise. Even though Mom continually bombarded us with criticism about our father, he never responded in kind. He answered our questions factually, but he never even hinted at any kind of criticism of her behavior or her life-style. He consistently reminded us that she was our mother and counseled us to love and honor her. As a result, I grew to love my dad more than I had ever thought possible, and I made up my mind that I would follow his example in dealing with people myself.

The same is true for the ordinances of the priesthood. When we value them and treat them with the reverence they deserve, our children come to more fully understand their importance as well. A single mother described the impact of her mother's positive example:

> I learned about the importance of the sacrament at a very early age. When I was six, my mother underwent emergency surgery. After returning home, she was bedridden for over a month. Each Sunday the priests in our ward came to our home and administered the sacrament. The first time they came, she cried when she partook of the bread. Later

31

she frequently told me how much the sacrament meant to her and described the spiritual strength she received from partaking of it. Since that time, I have had a special reverence for the emblems of the Lord's supper.

Children also learn to forgive by watching us forgive others. Sometimes that is much more challenging than we think. Consider the following example:

> While riding his bicycle home from elementary school one day, my little brother was accidentally hit by a car and killed. Later that evening my parents and I went to the home of the teenage driver of the car. The teenager had been hysterical because of what had happened.
>
> As soon as my dad saw the boy, he put his arms around him, hugged him to his breast, and said, "It was an accident. There is nothing you could have done to prevent it. We aren't angry with you. And we forgive you for what has happened." Everyone in that room wept. I will never forget the impact of that experience and my father's willingness to forgive a young man for taking the life of his son.

Seldom do we understand the extent to which setting a good example positively impacts our children's behavior. A mother of five children was delighted to learn of the long-term effect of one critical incident in her daughter's life:

> Twenty-two years ago, Carol was dating a young man whom she liked a great deal. One evening she told us that she would be home at 11:30 P.M. However, midnight came and went. By 3:30 A.M. she still wasn't home. I was terrified. I alternated between wanting to break her neck and praying that she was all right. At 4:00 A.M. I heard her slip into the house. I got out of bed, walked to the end of the hall, and waited. She turned around, looked at me, and said, "Oh, Mother, this has been the most spiritual night of my life. Frank has finally decided to go on a mission."
>
> Last week Carol sent us a letter in which she wrote, "You will never know how often I think about the night Frank decided to go on a mission and how understanding you were. You had every reason to be furious with me. But you

THE POWER OF EXAMPLE

listened. That single experience did more to help me understand what motherhood is all about than anything else you ever did."

Parents are the most important people in their children's lives. All our behaviors—whether benevolent or detrimental, accepting or critical, upbuilding or destructive, tender or harsh—have a powerful impact on our children's identities, self-esteem, and desires to live the gospel. They imitate us. What we do and what we are give a much more profound message than what we say. No greater service can be rendered to our children than for them to see the principles of the gospel manifest in our lives.

6

Children as Best Friends

As I walked past the restaurant, I looked through the window and saw Kathy standing next to the cashier. She smiled and waved, and I felt my stomach turn a little bit. Kathy was the vice president of our junior class, and I had caught her red-handed, skipping school. In the absence of a legitimate reason, I would, as the assistant principal, have to initiate disciplinary action against her. My first inclination was to pretend that I didn't see her; but it was too late, so I waited.

As she came out the restaurant door, I said, "Hi, Kathy. How are you doing?"

"Great. How are you?"

"Fine," I said. "How was lunch?"

"It was wonderful."

"Say, aren't you supposed to be in school?"

Kathy grinned at me and said, "Yup." She didn't appear to be the least bit concerned. If I had run into my assistant principal while skipping school, I would have been rattled.

"What's going on?" I asked.

"Oh, nothing much. I just decided to go to lunch with my best friend. I've got to hurry, though, or I'll be late for fifth period." I breathed a sigh of relief.

"That's neat. Who is your best friend?"

Again she smiled and said, "Excuse me just a minute, and I'll get her." Sixty seconds later Kathy emerged from the restaurant, arm in arm with a woman who looked as though she could

34

be her older sister. Kathy smiled and said, "I would like you to meet my mother. Mom, this is our assistant principal."

Being "Best Friends" with Our Children

Some parents strongly believe that developing friendships with their children is a mistake. They argue that the nature of parenting and the disciplinary process make it impossible to both be friends with their children and fulfill what they perceive to be their parental responsibilities. The disciplinary process alone requires objectivity; and objectivity with friends is impossible!

From our point of view, that is a dangerous and unwise notion. Those parents do not understand the powerful influence they can have on their children through friendship. As President Benson counseled, *"Take time to be a real friend to your children."*[1] Effective parenting is the process of righteously influencing children. When parents refuse to develop friendships with their children, they cut themselves off from their most powerful source of influence—the influence that comes from the high level of trust that exists between friends.

Trust is the single most important factor in healthy, interpersonal relationships. The degree to which people trust each other defines the nature of their relationship. Their trust for one another determines how much information they share, the extent to which they try to control others, and the degree to which they permit others to influence them.

To illustrate, a Sunday School teacher shared the following about a discussion with the twenty-two high school seniors in his class:

> After suggesting that each of my Sunday School students think about the person whom he or she trusted most in this world, I asked the following questions:
> • How much information do you share with that person? (The unanimous answer was "A lot.")
> • How much do you let that person influence you, in terms of following his or her counsel and advice? (Again, the unanimous answer was "A lot.")
> • How much do you try to control that person, particularly as it relates to protecting yourself against him or her? (Without exception, they said, "Very little.")

Then they identified, in their minds, the people they trusted the least, and I repeated the same three questions. Without exception, the students agreed that they shared little information with those people, and they permitted them to have virtually no influence on their lives. Further, they did everything they could to control the behavior of those untrustworthy people, particularly as it related to protecting themselves against them.

What is the difference between the two groups? Their interpersonal skills? Their communication skills? Their backgrounds? Their commitment to the gospel? It was none of those things. The difference was the degree to which they trusted the other people.

The basis of true friendship is trust, whether the friendship occurs inside or outside the family. Therefore, if parents want to be good friends with their children, they must behave in ways that foster their children's trust and confidence. When family members trust each other, almost everything in family life becomes easier, including teaching gospel principles. Consider the following experience of a concerned mother:

For several years my oldest daughter didn't trust her father. Although he is a wonderful husband, the chemistry just didn't seem to be "right" between the two of them. When she finally told me that she didn't trust him, mainly because of the way he talked to her in front of her friends, the lights went on for me and for my husband, and we finally had something specific to work on. Over the next six months, he did everything in his power to rebuild the trust he had lost. As my daughter later explained:

"My dad apologized to me, asked me to forgive him, and promised to never again criticize me in front of my friends. He also asked me to tell him about it if he ever slipped up and did it again. That hasn't been necessary because he hasn't slipped. We started holding covenant interviews [see chapter 16], and he kept every promise he made in those meetings as well. He also started to talk to me about the things I was doing that bugged him. By the way he did it, I could tell he was really interested. Whenever

36

I asked him for help, he would really help me, rather than finding fault with everything I did or telling me he was too busy. Soon I realized that he really meant it when he said he loved me, and I started to believe that he could be trusted."

The transformation in that girl was close to miraculous. She became more obedient. When my husband explained things to her, she listened—and then followed his counsel. Soon she began to seek his advice. Their relationship has become an enjoyable, rather than a painful one.

Our children will go to *someone* for advice in times of trouble. They will also ask *someone* for help when they need it. They are going to pattern their lives after *someone*. In short, *someone* is going to be our child's best friend. Why not nominate ourselves for the position of that someone?

Developing Friendships with Children

Developing friendships with our children can be a real challenge and, at best, a complex process. It requires a great deal of patience, primarily because proper parenting is a time-consuming process. It also takes time to build trust.

One thing, however, is absolutely essential: parents need to understand that developing friendships with their children does not come by dressing as they do, using teenage vernacular, or accompanying them everywhere they go. In short, parents don't become good friends with their children by acting like teenagers. Rather, friendships are built by following these prophetic guidelines, as given by President Benson: "Listen to your children, really listen. Talk with them, laugh and joke with them, sing with them, play with them, cry with them, hug them, honestly praise them. Yes, regularly spend unrushed one-on-one time with each child."[2] Friendships with our children come from treating them the same way we treat our good friends.

Several things can facilitate the process of building friendships with our children. For example, wise parents will stay as far away from criticism and fault-finding as possible. Research on behavioral change supports the idea that coercive and critical behavior provides very little motivation, except in the short run.

Criticism diminishes motivation, damages self-esteem, and almost always creates enemies, particularly in families. Consider,
for example, the following description by a grief-stricken mother:

> My husband has nearly destroyed his relationship with
> my son and daughter. In fact, they have told me on several
> occasions that they hate him. They can't seem to do any-
> thing right in his eyes. He is so mean and hateful. Every
> meal is a barrage of criticism and fault-finding. It has gotten
> to the point that the kids refuse to eat dinner with us; and
> they spend as much time away from home as possible. I
> have shed buckets of tears because of what is going on in
> our family, and I feel helpless to do anything about it. The
> irony is that he loves them very much and wants to help
> them, but he doesn't know how to go about it.

Unfortunately, the above example is repeated all too frequently. We have found that most people want to be successful
parents and that they are doing the best job they know how to
do. But many simply lack the necessary skills and knowledge.
Significant progress can be made, however, when parents understand that they will never motivate anyone by attacking them
with criticism. As one father explained:

> Am I motivated to excel when someone constantly tells
> me how rotten I am? Does telling my daughter how ugly
> she is help build her self-confidence and her interpersonal
> skills? Do I successfully motivate my son to do his school
> work when I tell him how stupid he is? Does that kind of
> treatment make me want to work extra hard and to go the
> extra mile? Absolutely not. It doesn't work with my kids;
> it doesn't work with my wife; and it doesn't work with me.
> All it does is build resentment and destroy self-confidence.
> The more I stay away from the negative, the more effective
> I am.

In building a "best friends" relationship with our children,
we need to realize the importance of keeping our priorities
straight. Note, for example, the lesson learned by a single mother
of four, three of whom were teenagers:

> My children have never been accused of being especially

tidy. In fact, sometimes they act like first-class slobs. They typically come home from school, dump their books and back packs on the floor, and then spend the afternoon watching TV or gabbing with each other.

Since I teach school, they usually get home before I do, and that means that I almost always walk into a pigpen. After a while I found myself caught in some win-lose dynamics, and I was losing! As soon as I walked through the front door, I immediately started my "Oh, my heavens" routine. The house was a mess. The kids hadn't practiced the piano. They also hadn't done their homework. So I put on my "Hitler hat" and got them moving.

Pretty soon I noticed that they stopped looking forward to me coming home. In fact, they resented my presence. That quickly got my attention. I felt that I should be concerned about the school work, the piano practice, the condition of the house, and their discipline. However, I realized that it was an issue of *timing*.

Now when I come home, I intentionally ignore everything except the personal needs of my children. I try to have a private talk with each child. Sometimes it's for ten minutes; sometimes it's only for two, depending on the need of the child. I ask them how their day went. "What happened that was good and what happened that was lousy today?" We rejoice together in the successes and think about what to do with the problems.

Then after supper I'll say, "Okay, you guys, I need fifteen minutes of slave labor, and we'll set the timer." We quickly put away the books, clean up the mess in the living room, and do whatever we need to make the place presentable. Most of the time it is fun for all of us. But I first get in touch with them personally and emotionally. I find that that works much better than coming home and criticizing them for just being kids.

If you are ever tempted to criticize or condemn your child, take the time to read the following article, "Father Forgets," written many years ago by W. Livingston Larned. Time has proven it to be one of those rare gems that continue to strike a chord in hearts of subsequent generations.

Listen, son: I am saying this as you lie asleep, one little paw crumpled under your cheek and the blond curls stickily wet on your damp forehead. I have stolen into your room alone. Just a few minutes ago, as I sat reading my paper in the library, a stifling wave of remorse swept over me. Guiltily I came to your bedside.

These are the things I have been thinking, son: I had been cross to you. I scolded you as you were dressing for school because you gave your face merely a dab with a towel. I took you to task for not cleaning your shoes. I called out angrily when you threw some of your things on the floor.

At breakfast I found fault, too. You spilled things. You gulped down your food. You put your elbows on the table. You spread butter too thick on your bread. And as you started off to play and I made for my train, you turned and waved a hand and called, "Good-bye, Daddy!" and I frowned, and said in reply, "Hold your shoulders back!"

Then it began all over again in the late afternoon. As I came up the road I spied you, down on your knees, playing marbles. There were holes in your stockings. I humiliated you before your boyfriends by marching you ahead of me to the house. Stockings were expensive—and if you had to buy them you would be more careful! Imagine that, son, from a father!

Do you remember, later, when I was reading in the library, how you came in, timidly, with a sort of hurt look in your eyes? When I glanced up over my paper, impatient at the interruption, you hesitated at the door. "What is it you want?" I snapped. You said nothing, but ran across in one tempestuous plunge, and threw your arms around my neck and kissed me, and your small arms tightened with an affection that God had set blooming in your heart and which even neglect could not wither. And then you were gone, pattering up the stairs.

Well, son, it was shortly afterwards that my paper slipped from my hands and a terrible sickening fear came over me. What has habit been doing to me? The habit of finding fault, of reprimanding—this was my reward to you for being a boy. It was not that I did not love you; it was that I expected too much of youth. I was measuring you by the yardstick of my own years.

And there was so much that was good and fine and true in your character. The little heart of you was as big as the dawn itself over the wide hills. This was shown by your spontaneous impulse to rush in and kiss me goodnight. Nothing else matters tonight, son. I have come to your bedside in the darkness, and I have knelt there, ashamed!

It is a feeble atonement; I know you would not understand these things if I told them to you during your waking hours. But tomorrow I will be a real daddy! I will chum with you, and suffer when you suffer, and laugh when you laugh. I will bite my tongue when impatient words come. I will keep saying as if it were a ritual: "He is nothing but a boy—a little boy."

I am afraid I have visualized you as a man. Yet as I see you now, son, crumpled and weary in your cot, I see that you are still a baby. Yesterday you were in your mother's arms, your head on her shoulder. I have asked too much, too much.[3]

Friendships are built when we treat our children with respect and accept them as they are in their various stages of progress. One father benefited from some insight about the matter that his teenage daughter gave him:

My fourteen-year-old daughter's best friend is an unusual girl. In fact, some people think she's weird. She was the only girl to play on the boys' eighth-grade football team. For two years she wore shoes and socks that didn't match; and many aspects of her behavior were as unique as her appearance. She is the last girl I would have suspected my daughter to pal around with. When I asked my daughter what she liked about her friend, she said, "I can tell her anything, and she never judges me. She never criticizes me. She never tells me how stupid I am for feeling a certain way or for doing some of the things I do. It's really safe to be with her and to talk to her. I feel important when I'm with her." That was a great lesson for me, and I realized that if I wanted to be good friends with my daughter, I had better start treating her at least as well as her friends treat her.

In short, if we want to be friends with our children, we need to treat them the same way we treat good friends. We must let them know that we value and appreciate them, and we must provide the support and encouragement they need to become healthy and responsible adults.

That kind of growth is best accomplished in a supportive and positive atmosphere. Why? Because that is the way people grow—toward light and warmth, toward the positive. Children thrive in that kind of an environment, and they trust those who provide such a climate. When children know that their parents value and appreciate them, they usually see their parents as friends—even when corrective action is taken. And remember that children and parents, as friends do everywhere, take special efforts to make their friends happy.

However, recognizing our children as friends and developing those friendships take time. Establishing a friendship requires spending time with them when they need it, whether or not it is convenient. Sometimes, though, it is at the most inconvenient times that the investment of time yields the greatest returns. One father recalled this great experience with his seventeen-year-old son:

> Richard arrived home on Sunday at 1:30 A.M. after attending a musical workshop in another state. As always, he let me know he was home as soon as he arrived. I got up, staggered to the kitchen table, poured him a glass of milk, and broke open a package of chocolate chip cookies. Then I sat down at the kitchen table and listened.
>
> Richard shared the details of each day's activities and talked excitedly about the girls he had met. He described, with some embarrassment mixed with pride, the pranks he and his roommates had engineered. He also explained how he had spent one evening defending the Prophet Joseph Smith, the Word of Wisdom, and the law of chastity. At 3:15 A.M., he paused, looked at me, and said, "You know what, Dad? I honestly think that you like me."

42

"What on earth gave you that idea?"

"Look at it this way." His eyes became moist. "I wake you out of a deep sleep at 1:30 in the morning. You get up, listen to me yak for almost two hours, and even act as if you're really interested. There's no way you would do that if you didn't really care for somebody. I really believe that I'm very important to you."

I smiled and responded, "Are you really important to me? My son, you have no idea."

Parenting is not an easy task. But by treating our children the way we treat our best friends, we avoid the trap of letting "the things that matter most . . . [be] at the mercy of things that matter least."[4] Besides, being friends with our children is an extremely enjoyable way to be parents.

7

The Good
Neighbor Policy

*As I pulled the car into the driveway, I immediately knew
that I was in trouble. The living room light was still on, which
meant that my dad was still awake. And only one thing would
keep him up until 1:30 A.M.: his sixteen-year-old son was in
trouble. But it had to be a coincidence; nobody could have found
out what we had done!*

*As I opened the front door, Dad put down the newspaper,
smiled, and said, "Hi, Son. How's it going?"*

*I swallowed and tried to act relaxed. "Great. How are you
doing?"*

*"Have a seat. I'd like to chat with you for a minute." I sat
down. "Anything unusual happen tonight?"*

*"What do you mean?" Secretly I suspected I had been found
out.*

*He looked at me with that half-smile that meant he knew
more than he was telling me and again asked, "Anything unusual
happen tonight?"*

"We did a lot of things."

*"That's what I understand. I talked with Sheriff Roder earlier
this evening. Would you like to tell me what happened?"*

*"Sheriff Roder is a jerk—a typical small town cop. He hates
us, and he won't leave us alone. They ought to fire him. He
deserves all the garbage he gets."*

"Would you like to tell me what happened?"

By now I was certain that he knew all about it. "Gary, Jack, and I were driving around, talking about nothing like we do sometimes. When we drove passed Sheriff Roder's house, we saw those yellow rose bushes in his garden next to the road. Jack said it would be great to get back at him for all the junk he's given to us. Nobody was around, and the lights in his house were out. So I pulled the car into his rose garden, revved up the motor, popped the clutch, and peeled out. I think we got a few of his rose bushes." I smiled with pleasure.

"That's close to the story I got. However, you wiped out more than just a few of them. Sheriff Roder watched the whole thing from his living-room window."

"You're kidding!" Suddenly it didn't seem all that funny anymore.

"He got your license-plate number, and a few minutes later he rang our doorbell. We really had quite an interesting visit. By the way, he'd like to visit with you in his office at eight o'clock in the morning." I could feel myself getting sick. "Would you like to talk about it?"

I took a deep breath. "Not right now."

Dad said, "Well, why don't you sleep on it. If you'd like to visit in the morning before your meeting, I'll be available. It looks as if you've got yourself a serious problem. It'll be interesting to see how you handle it." As I stood up, I felt my knees weaken. Dad gave me my nightly hug, said good night, and went to bed.

The whole thing was admirable. No yelling. No threats. No criticism. No overreaction. Just a simple, respectful discussion of the problem — exactly the way he talked to our neighbor after his daughter lost control of their family car and knocked down ten feet of our fence. It would be tough to face Sheriff Roder, but Dad knew I could handle it, so I was left to face the consequences of my behavior.

Love Thy Neighbor as Thyself

Luke records that a lawyer asked the Lord, "What shall I do to inherit eternal life?" Jesus asked in turn, "What is written in the law?" and then agreed with the lawyer's response: "Thou shalt love the Lord thy God with all thy heart, and with all thy soul, and with all thy strength, and with all thy mind; and thy

45

neighbor as thyself." (Luke 10:25–27.) Then the lawyer asked, "Who is my neighbor?" Jesus responded with the parable of the good Samaritan, admonishing the man, "Go, and do thou likewise." (Luke 10:29, 37.)

Since the Savior even included complete strangers in his definition of "neighbors," we can safely assume that members of our own families are also neighbors. Something as simple as treating our family members as we treat our good neighbors can have a wonderful effect on our children. As Foster Cline explains,

> The Good Neighbor Policy is . . . so sensible that it seems like nonsense; so thoughtful that it may seem non-caring; so friendly that it may seem non-parental. When parents follow the Good Neighbor Policy, they almost inevitably raise friendly children. They raise children who will turn out to be Good Neighbors! Because children learn almost all things through modeling, it means that *if parents want their children to grow up to be good neighbors, they must treat their children like good neighbors.*[1]

As good neighbors, we show concern for people, we do what we can to help them, we keep our noses out of their business unless we are asked for advice, and we let them experience the consequences of their actions. These same behaviors can also help us rear healthy, responsible children, because the principles relate directly to most of the normal problems that children encounter.

The Good Neighbor Policy can be applied in a variety of different ways.[2] For example, if my neighbor borrowed my lawn mower and then ran over a large rock, damaging the blade, which of the following would I (as a good neighbor) say?

• "Good grief, John, I can't believe you're so irresponsible. Didn't it occur to you to pick up the rocks before you mowed the lawn? This is the last time I'll ever loan you anything, so if you're thinking about borrowing something else from me, forget it."

• "Do you think I'm made of money? I can't afford this type of expense! I can't believe you'd be so careless and irresponsible with something that isn't even yours!"

• "This is the last straw. You've pushed me too far this time. You're grounded from all privileges, and you can't borrow anything from me again for two months!"

• "Hey, John, that's too bad. But those things happen sometimes. When do you plan to get it fixed?"

Of course, the last answer is the most appropriate. In fact, the first three alternatives seem so preposterous that they're almost absurd; any one of them would only exaggerate the problem and seriously damage the relationship.

Most of us go out of our way to be friendly and cordial with our neighbors. Very seldom do we get angry with them when they make mistakes that don't directly affect us; and even when a mistake may affect us, we try to be tolerant and understanding. We accept their idiosyncrasies. If they're having problems, even if they've caused the problems themselves, we feel concern about their plight. Sometimes, when asked, we offer advice. We also provide support, and we help when we can.

However, when it comes to our own children, we often forget that the same laws apply. We tend to overreact. We may scream, yell, threaten, and intimidate them. As a result, we temporarily — and sometimes permanently — damage our relationships with them. They may begin to distrust us or put up defensive walls. Then we become perplexed when our children talk not to us but to others about their problems. Children confide in people who treat them with respect and who value their friendship. The simple truth is that family members would have many more friends inside the family if they treated each other the way they treated their good neighbors.

Applying the Good Neighbor Policy doesn't mean ignoring problems. Even when children make decisions that are harmful to themselves, there are ways we can be of help and still maintain a healthy, trusting relationship with them. Consider the following example:

> During the second quarter of the seventh grade, Nate came home with a midquarter grade of D- in math. Since aptitude tests had consistently placed him in the 98th percentile, and since he received an A- his first quarter, this

47

report got my undivided attention. Therefore, I invited myself to a meeting with Nate and his teacher. When I asked about the poor grade, Mrs. Jackson explained, "Nate has the ability, all right. But he's lazy. He talks during the entire class period, and he doesn't turn in his homework."

Nate looked at me with an expression on his face that said, "Okay, now you know. What are you doing to do about it?"

"Nate, is that correct?"

"Yup," he said with a smile.

"So what do we do about it?" I asked.

Mrs. Jackson answered, "I don't know. I've tried everything that I can think of. He simply won't respond."

"Nate, what do you think we ought to do about it?"

"I don't know, Dad. Math isn't fun any more. It's a royal pain. Besides, I have other things to do."

"Well, it sounds as if you have a problem. You see, seventh-grade math is very important, because it's the foundation for all the math classes you take the rest of your life. In fact, it's so important for you to understand the basics that you can't progress without it.

"Now, the only way I know how to determine if you understand the material is to look at your grades. Therefore, if you don't get at least a B in the class, it means you don't understand the material well enough to go on to eighth-grade math. So you'll have the unique opportunity to take seventh-grade math again as an eighth grader." Nate turned white.

"Mrs. Jackson, do you have any eighth graders taking seventh-grade math right now?"

"Yes. One boy is taking it, and he hates it."

"Well, Nate, it seems that you have some decisions to make. I'm curious to see how it all turns out. If I can be of any help, let me know." I then thanked Mrs. Jackson, and we left.

Within one week Nate's math grade jumped to a B +. He got an A for the quarter, and he has excelled in the subject ever since.

Most of the time children know when they have made a

mistake. When parents refuse to overreact and, at the same time, let children take responsibility for their own difficulties, the problems almost always get resolved. In the process, healthy parent-child relationships are maintained because mutual trust is built up, and self-confidence increases because children develop the ability to solve their own problems.

Children need a safe environment in which it's okay to make mistakes. In such an environment, they realize that they can talk about their problems and learn to deal with them without the fear of always being punished. If we continually punish children for telling us the truth, then we are really training children to lie to us. In short, parents need to make it safe for kids to share their concerns without the fear of being humiliated or embarrassed.

Of course, some problems are more serious than others; and sometimes problems arise that are very expensive to resolve. Even in those cases, the natural consequences the child faces because of those problems are usually enough to teach them sufficiently. Thus, the Good Neighbor Policy still applies, as illustrated by the experience of a father of three teenagers:

> Our house was full of excitement that afternoon. Eric had the lead part in the school musical, which was opening tonight in less than three hours. Tomorrow was also Eric's eighteenth birthday, and true to form, he was trying to finish the last requirements for his Eagle Scout Award before the deadline.
>
> As I sat on the living-room couch talking with my youngest son, I heard the back door slam. "Dad, can I talk with you for a minute? It's important!"
>
> I walked into the kitchen and saw Eric, standing by the back door, his face flushed. "Hi, Eric. What's up?"
>
> "I just wrecked the car."
>
> "Are you okay?" I asked anxiously.
>
> "Yes."
>
> "Was anyone hurt?"
>
> "No. But the front end of the car is all smashed up."
>
> "What happened?"
>
> It had been snowing all day, and the streets were ex-

tremely slick. While driving through a parking lot at less than five m.p.h., Eric put on the brakes. Unfortunately, the car slid underneath the back bumper of a pickup truck. The truck didn't get a scratch, but the front end of our car was wrecked.

We walked out to the driveway and looked at the car. I quietly estimated the cost of the damage at roughly fifteen hundred dollars. But I forced myself to smile and said, "Well, the front end has developed some *real character* since I last saw it."

"Yeah, I guess it has. You know, Dad, this is really embarrassing. Here I am, passing off my safety merit badge for my Eagle Scout Award, and I get in a wreck! What am I going to tell people?"

I was actually tempted to laugh. "Listen, Son, nobody was hurt, and that's the important thing."

"Won't our insurance rates go up?"

"Probably. We'll have to see. But we have more important things to worry about right now."

"Am I in trouble?"

"Did you mean to wreck the car?"

"No."

"Of course not. Accidents happen to all of us. We'll have to get the car fixed, but we can talk about the details later."

"Thanks, Dad."

Later that evening, after the musical had finished, I talked with the director. "Congratulations on how well your son did," she said.

"Thank you. He really enjoys it."

"I understand you had a little excitement around your house tonight. I don't know all the details of what happened, but Eric announced to the entire cast that he had just wrecked the family car. The kids all laughed, and then one of them said, 'I'll bet your parents were furious.'

"Eric said, 'No, they're not the least bit miffed.'

" 'You mean they didn't yell at you?' asked another.

" 'Nope.'

" 'Are you grounded?'

" 'Nope.'

50

" 'Are you going to have to pay for the damage?'

" 'I'm sure I will,' Eric said. 'I'll also have to pay the increased insurance premiums. But they didn't yell at me, and I didn't get into trouble. My dad just said that he was glad that nobody got hurt, and we can talk about the details later.'

" 'Sounds like you've got some great folks.'

"Eric smiled and said, 'Yeah, they're awesome.'

"The kids couldn't believe it. None of them had ever had that kind of an experience with their parents. You really have a remarkable relationship with that boy. Few kids are so fortunate."

Taking time to think about the Good Neighbor Policy before we react can help us handle problems in a way that will prepare our children to become successful adults. Parents who consistently apply that policy in their homes find that their children grow up to behave like good neighbors, both inside and outside the family. Being good neighbors and treating others as good neighbors makes it much easier to love our neighbors as ourselves, particularly those neighbors who live within the walls of our own homes.

8

Teaching Children Obedience

"Dad, people always talk about spiritual experiences, but I don't get any. In fact, I've never had a revelation in my life."

That seemed like a legitimate concern for a fifteen-year-old boy. I was delighted that my son was finally ready to talk about such things. "Are you sure about that?" I asked.

"Sure, I'm sure."

"Why do you think that's the case?"

"I don't know. I understand the gospel pretty well, but spiritual experiences still aren't coming. Do you have any ideas?"

"Maybe," I said. "Mind if I ask you some questions?"

"Be my guest."

"How often do you read the scriptures privately — not with us as a family, but on your own?"

"Almost never."

"What about your prayers? Do you pray privately?"

"Not much anymore. I used to pray all the time, but I never got anything out of it. So I quit."

"How do you feel about going to church?"

"It's okay, I guess. I know I ought to, but it gets pretty boring."

"Do you go to early morning seminary?"

"Dad, you know I don't!"

I smiled. "Now that I think about it, you're right." I reached for the scriptures and read aloud the following: "There is a law, irrevocably decreed in heaven before the foundations of this world, upon which all blessings are predicated — and when we obtain any blessing from God, it is by obedience to that law upon which it is predicated." [D&C 130:20–21.]

I then said, "There's no reason whatsoever for you to be having spiritual experiences. You're not doing anything to receive them. You're only going through the motions, and that's not enough. Spiritual experiences will come when you decide to follow the Lord's program, and not until then. You say you want the Lord's blessings, but only on your terms, not his. Fortunately, that isn't the way the Lord works."

"That's not what happened to Alma and Paul. They didn't keep all the commandments, but the Lord gave them great manifestations anyway."

"True, they had their visions. But notice what they experienced. The angel didn't say to Alma, 'Behold, because of your faithfulness, you are about to have a wonderful, spiritual experience. Listen to the will of the Lord, and learn about the great mysteries of the kingdom.' What the angel said was, 'Seek to destroy the church no more' [Mosiah 27:16], and then he called Alma to repentance. In effect, the angel said, 'Look, if you want to destroy yourself, that's your business, and you have the freedom to do so; but stop trying to destroy the church of God in the process.' You remember how Alma suffered for two days and two nights?

"That's basically the same message the Savior gave to Paul. He said, 'Why persecutest thou me?' [Acts 9:4.] Paul had been having a problem seeing clearly with his natural eyes, but things came more into focus after he was blind for a while. He got a much different outlook on life. You see, Son, both Alma and Paul went through literal hell before they became instruments in God's hands."

"So it all hinges on obedience?"

"That's right. You have the freedom not to pray, not to study the scriptures, not to worship at church. It's your choice. But don't expect to be rewarded for doing so. If, on the other hand, you choose to keep the commandments, your Father in Heaven will bless you with the spiritual experiences you seek. It's up to you."

Teach Children to Obey the Lord's Commandments

Obedience is the key to personal righteousness and progression. It is also the key to personal revelation, to happiness, to freedom, and to a host of other blessings. Elder L. Tom Perry said, "The most important inner quality you can instill in a child is faith in God; *the most important action a child can learn is obedience;* the most powerful tool you have with which to teach a child is love."[1] Obedience involves action. It is not enough to merely understand it. We must do it!

In teaching our children, most of us find that it is one thing to teach them the principles of the gospel, and it is something else to instill within them a desire to obey those principles. *How* we teach them obedience strongly influences their desire to obey their Father in Heaven. That is why Marion G. Romney wisely gave the following caution:

> Whatever our method, however, we should remember that our teaching, to be successful and effective, must convince our children that living the gospel is the way to happiness. If they feel that the discipline, attitudes, and practices to which they are subject are arbitrary, that without reason they restrict their activities and keep them from enjoying life, they will conform only so long as we have them under our immediate influence.[2]

When obedience is an enjoyable and rewarding experience, children learn to love the Lord and desire to keep his commandments. If, on the other hand, obedience becomes painful and restrictive, children will learn to hate the commandments and see them as unacceptable guidelines for behavior. When we make living the gospel enjoyable and fruitful, children are better able to learn first-hand that obedience need not be drudgery, that it need not be painful, and that it need not be restrictive.

As a junior in high school reported, "Ever since I was little, I have found it fun to live the gospel. I'm not sure what my parents did to teach that to me, but I have more freedom, greater opportunities, and fewer serious problems than my friends. I also feel more comfortable making mistakes, because I know that I have my family's support. Whatever I want to do that's worthwhile, they do all they can to help me."

We have a unique opportunity to make life either enjoyable or miserable for our children. The latter, unfortunately, is easy to do. If we continually criticize, badger, and nag them for not doing this or that, they will be miserable and devalue the things that are important to us. If, on the other hand, we support our children and show them the power of obedience in our own lives, they are more likely to value the things we see as important. We have the power to create either kind of climate. In this context, a young mother explained,

> My husband and I fully understand that it's our responsibility as parents to create the right atmosphere for our children to grow and develop. So we work hard to make living the gospel an enjoyable experience. For example, we have fun going to and from church and singing the hymns. Even though we don't have much control over the sacrament meeting speakers, the little ones can quietly draw pictures, as long as they remain reverent. If attending church is a positive experience, they will want to keep going.
> We also try to make family home evenings enjoyable. That means activities, music, lessons, and love. Learning the gospel doesn't have to be boring. When we teach our children gospel principles, we try to do it in a way that holds their attention. That doesn't mean that we water down the doctrine; we just try to make it entertaining. The bottom line is that we try to reward them for their obedience, knowing full well that the behaviors that get rewarded are the behaviors that continue. It is more of an attitude than anything in particular.

When learning is an enjoyable experience, children find it easier to remember gospel principles. Studying the gospel becomes more rewarding for them. For example, a mother of three reported how well she remembers one lesson her father delivered. The environment in which it was given was critical to how effectively it was understood.

> From as early as I can remember, my father was either a bishop or a stake president. Fortunately, his job allowed

him the flexibility to be with us every morning for breakfast. Each morning one of us selected his or her favorite scripture story, and Dad then read them to us, often dramatizing the story and hamming it up just a bit.

One morning he talked about Helaman's discussion with his son Corianton. I will never forget how I felt when Dad read the following words: "Behold, O my son, how great iniquity ye brought upon the Zoramites; for when they saw your conduct they would not believe in my words." [Alma 39:11.] He explained that the behavior of *every* member of our family determined whether he would be a successful stake president and whether the members would believe what he told them. I have never forgotten that important lesson, and since then I have wanted to keep the commandments. I knew my father loved me, and I didn't want to let him down.

There are also key times when children are especially receptive to learning the lessons of obedience. The times just before priesthood ordinances are performed are such occasions. Consider, for example, the experience that a father of two children had with his own father:

Before my baptism and ordinations to the various offices in the priesthood, Dad sat down with me and explained the responsibilities and obligations I was about to take upon myself. In each of these conversations, he said something like "Now, Son, this is an important step in your life. Once you participate in this ordinance, your Father in Heaven will expect much more from you than he has in the past because you've made covenants with him that require greater levels of obedience. With this ordinance also come greater blessings from the Lord. But you must fulfill your responsibilities and keep your covenants in order to get them. All of the blessings associated with this ordinance depend upon your obedience to the commandments. So if you aren't willing to be obedient to the commandments, don't participate in the ordinance." The genius of those discussions was that they took place *before* the ordinance was performed, and I was given a choice. Each time I chose to participate, which meant that I also chose to keep the commandments. But my commitment to do so came first. That made all the difference in the world.

Despite the wickedness that exists in the world today, living the gospel becomes easier when children understand and accept the fact that obedience is not always convenient. As one mother explained,

> I continuously explain to my kids that the Lord did not guarantee that living the gospel would always be either fun or convenient, which is one of the major reasons some of their friends both inside and outside the Church don't always keep the commandments. Children constantly have to choose between living celestial or telestial laws. The joy that comes from living celestial laws will not come easily, but it will come.

Thus, teaching children obedience can be challenging. However, there are some basic things that we can do to help our children gain the desire to keep the commandments. A mother of four described her parents' method in the following way:

> There were three things that contributed to my *wanting* to keep the commandments. First, my folks kept the commandments themselves. They set the example for me. They didn't ask me to do something they didn't do themselves. Second, they expected me to keep the commandments. Third, they loved me. There was never any doubt in my mind about that. And I loved them as well. It is always easier to follow someone who does the right thing and loves you.

Teaching the principle of obedience should begin at the earliest age possible. President Joseph Fielding Smith said:

> Of course there should be prayer and faith and love and obedience to God in the home. It is the duty of parents to teach their children these saving principles of the gospel of Jesus Christ, so that they will know why they are to be baptized and that they may be impressed in their hearts with a desire to continue to keep the commandments of

God after they are baptized, that they may come back into his presence. Do you, my good brethren and sisters, want your families, your children; do you want to be sealed to your fathers and your mothers before you? . . . If so, then you must begin by teaching at the cradle-side. You are to teach by example as well as precept.[3]

Obedience to the Lord's commandments brings spiritual power into our lives, and under such conditions, we can enjoy profound spiritual experiences. Every devoted member of the Church has the right to receive revelation from the Lord. The Prophet Joseph Smith said, "No man can receive the Holy Ghost without receiving revelations. The Holy Ghost is a revelator."[4] Therefore, we need to help our children understand the great blessings that come from obedience to the laws and ordinances of the gospel and teach them how to receive the revelations God has promised. As the Lord said, "I, the Lord, am bound when ye do what I say." (D&C 82:10.) When our children are obedient, they place themselves in a position to call upon the powers of heaven.

9

Follow the Brethren

My father took his place at the pulpit and looked over the congregation for a full thirty seconds without saying a word. Finally he spoke. "As you are aware, there has been a lot of talk lately about our new bishop and whether he's really qualified to serve. Well, I think we have a lot of evidence that he isn't. He's too young, and he has had no administrative experience. I am equally certain that I am the most qualified man in this ward to serve as your bishop."

Less than a month had passed since the new bishop was sustained, and the gossip was rampant. The bishop, who had grown up in our community, was twenty-five years old and had been married only a year. Most of the ward members had watched him grow up. Some had even been his baby-sitters. They had tolerated his irreverence and put up with his rudeness and pranks. Now he was their bishop.

Today was our first regular testimony meeting since the new bishopric was installed. For the first ten minutes, nobody said a word. Then Dad had walked to the pulpit. It was one of those events that I will never forget.

Dad continued speaking. "Let me tell you why I am the most qualified man to serve as bishop. I have been an administrator all my professional life, and I'm good at it. I've already been a bishop once. I've been on the stake high council and also held other responsible stake and ward positions. I love the youth in this ward and have a good relationship with them. I also know almost everyone here today very well; I love you dearly and feel the same measure of love in return. Furthermore, I have a Ph.D. Therefore, I submit to you that nobody is more qualified than I am to serve as your bishop."

Nobody moved a muscle. Every eye was riveted on the pulpit. The babies didn't even cry. Dad then said, "But as you are aware, I wasn't called. Why? Because decisions like that aren't made on the basis of someone's outward qualifications. Bishops are called by revelation. So it doesn't matter whether our new bishop meets my own private set of standards. He is obviously qualified, or he wouldn't have been selected. The Lord called him to lead us, and I sustain him in that call. Furthermore, I pledge my support to him and will also do everything in my power to help him succeed." He then bore his testimony about the truthfulness of the gospel and sat down.

Supporting Church Leaders

President David O. McKay said, "The greatest safeguard we have for unity and strength in the Church is found in the priesthood, by honoring and respecting it."[1] It follows, then, that we have the sacred obligation to teach our children to support and to sustain Church leaders. Without the conviction that leaders are called by revelation, a member could not fully support them. Indeed, a member's spiritual survival depends on that conviction, for there will always be detractors whose purpose is to destroy faith and undermine the Church. The father of a sixteen-year-old boy recounted the following experience:

> Recently the father of Bill, my son's best friend, had some serious problems with the Church. As a result, my son, a sophomore in high school, was continuously bombarded with criticism about the Church. Although he lacked the background to effectively address the man's concerns, he didn't hesitate to stand up for the truth. The positive side of it was that these challenges provided numerous opportunities for my son and me to have some lengthy gospel discussions.

> After one particularly confronting evening, my son raised some interesting questions. "Dad, what about blind obedience?"

"Sounds like you had a pretty tough night," I responded.
"It was awful. I didn't know what to say to him."

I reached for a recent copy of the *Ensign*. "This might help. Let me read you something that Elder Packer said in general conference: 'Latter-day Saints are not obedient because they are compelled to be obedient. They are obedient because they know certain spiritual truths and have decided, as an expression of their own individual agency, to obey the commandments of God. . . . Those who talk of blind obedience may appear to know many things, but they do not understand the doctrines of the gospel. There is an obedience that comes from a knowledge of the truth that transcends any external form of control. We are not obedient because we are blind, we are obedient because we can see.'[2] The Lord never expects blind obedience from anyone. We can go to him at any time and get the answers that we desire."

"But Dad, his arguments sound so logical. When I tell him I know the gospel is true, he just laughs at me. How can you tell the difference between someone who is really struggling to know the truth and someone who is out to undermine the Church?"

"There are several ways. First, Jesus said in 3 Nephi 11:29, 'He that hath the spirit of contention is not of me, but is of the devil.' That tells us something about who's behind an argument. Second, Elder Packer said that 'two things characterize [antagonists]: they are always irritated by the word *obedience*, and always they question revelation.' "[3]

"But Dad, we know that Church leaders aren't perfect. Bill's dad said it's foolish to follow someone when he's made a mistake."

"Yes, our leaders sometimes do make mistakes. But we have a sacred responsibility to follow them anyway."

"How is that different from obeying blindly?"

"Brigham Young said that he once found himself being critical of the way the Prophet Joseph handled some financial matters. Even though those thoughts lasted less than sixty seconds, the 'spirit of revelation manifested to [him] that if [he] was to harbor a thought in [his] heart that Joseph could be wrong in anything, [he] would begin to lose confidence in him' to the point that he could not believe anything that Joseph said. Brigham concluded, 'Though I [knew] that Joseph was a human being and subject to err, still it was none of my business to look after his faults. . . . It was not my prerogative to call him in question with regard to any act of his life. He was God's servant, and not mine.'[4] You see, Brigham Young understood that you cannot criticize God's prophet without criticizing God.''

"Does that mean we just ignore mistakes, even if they're serious?"

"Son, let me give you another example. Assume for just a minute that you and some of your friends are climbing a mountain. It's a dangerous undertaking, so you tie a rope around each of your waists to protect yourselves, just in case someone falls. The leader of the group is an excellent mountain climber. He has climbed this mountain many times before, and he knows the way. Now suppose you're almost to the top when the leader steps on something he thinks is solid, only to find that it isn't. He slips, and there he is, hanging over the edge from the rope.

"What is your responsibility? Do you say, 'I can't believe it. You're supposed to be our leader. You're supposed to know the way. How could anyone be so stupid as to slip and fall like that in front of everybody? You obviously don't deserve to lead this group!' So you take out a pocket knife, cut the rope, and say, 'So long!' "

"Dad, that's sick!"

"Of course it's sick. It's also obvious what you'd do. You'd pull him back up, make certain that he's okay, and encourage him to continue leading you. Why? Because in spite of his mistake, he's still the best qualified person to help you reach the top."

"Okay. I have another question. The Prophet Joseph said that a prophet is only a prophet when he's acting as such. How do you know whether the President of the Church is speaking as a prophet or as just a man?"

"Son, I've found that if you apply two simple tests, you'll

never be deceived. First, the statement will be consistent with what's taught in the scriptures. Second, the Spirit will bear witness to you that the doctrine is true. You have the right to receive a spiritual witness from the Lord about the truthfulness of any doctrine taught, regardless of the source. These are just two of the safeguards the Lord has prepared against deception."

When the prophet of the Lord speaks, children have a right to know that he is speaking for and in behalf of their Heavenly Father. That means that neither parents nor their children should ever find fault with the Lord's prophet. The same principle applies to local authorities as well. As President McKay said, "It is one of the most poisonous things that can be introduced into the home of a Latter-day Saint—this murmuring against presidents of stakes, high councilors, Sunday School superintendents, presidents of high priests' quorums, seventies, elders, priests, teachers, and deacons."[5] President Gordon B. Hinkley also warned us against criticism of local leaders:

> Unless there is loyalty toward the bishop and stake president on a local level, there will be an absence of harmony, there will be suspicion and hesitation to serve with fidelity, there will be that kind of division which is always destructive of faith. Let it ever be remembered that no President of this church, no counselor in the Presidency, no General Authority, no member of a stake presidency or of a bishopric or of an elders quorum presidency is there because he wished to be there and requested the privilege. Each is there because he was "called of God, by prophecy, and by the laying on of hands by those who are in authority, to preach the Gospel and administer in the ordinances thereof." (A of F 5.) Loyalty to leadership is a cardinal requirement of all who serve in the army of the Lord. A house divided against itself cannot stand. (See Mark 3:25.) Unity is basic and essential.[6]

Thus, parents who find fault with their leaders place themselves and their children in a very dangerous position. As Dallin H. Oaks explained, "The primary reason we are commanded to avoid criticism is to preserve our own spiritual well-being, not to protect the person whom we would criticize."[7] The following experience of a bishop illustrates the point:

> Several months ago I talked with a man who was offended by something our stake president had said to him. After he told me his side of the story, I said, "If that had happened to me, and I had the same background and experience you have had, I suspect that I'd feel the same way you do. Have you talked with him about this?"
>
> "No."
>
> "Why not?" I asked.
>
> "Because it won't do any good. He doesn't listen."
>
> "I suggest that you talk with him. If you choose not to do that, then I suggest that you forgive him, forget about this whole matter, and get on with living."
>
> "Why would I do that?"
>
> "The Church means a lot to you, doesn't it?"
>
> "Yes. It's my life."
>
> "When you criticize the stake president," I said, "you are really undermining the Church."
>
> "That's nonsense. He's a public official. It comes with the territory. If he makes a mistake, I have a right to call him on it."
>
> "There is a difference between Church officials and other public figures. Let me read you something Elder Dallin H. Oaks said: 'Criticism is particularly objectionable when it is directed toward Church authorities, general or local. Jude condemns those who "speak evil of dignities" (Jude 1:8). Evil speaking of the Lord's anointed is in a class by itself. It is one thing to depreciate a person who exercises corporate power or even government power. It is quite another thing to criticize or depreciate a person for the performance of an office to which he or she has been called of God. It does not matter that the criticism is true. As Elder George F. Richards, President of the Council of the Twelve, said in a conference in April 1947, "When we say anything bad about the leaders of the Church, whether true or false, we tend to impair their influence and their usefulness and are thus working against the Lord and his cause." '[8]

"Don't give me that stuff. You're just trying to protect him."

"Not so. Listen to the rest of the statement: 'The counsel against speaking evil of Church leaders is not so much for the benefit of the leaders as it is for the spiritual well-being of members who are prone to murmur and find fault. The Church leaders I know are durable people. They made their way successfully in a world of unrestrained criticism before they received their current callings. They have no personal need for protection; they seek no personal immunities from criticism—constructive or destructive. They only seek to declare what they understand to be the word of the Lord to his people.'[9]

"If you continue to murmur and find fault, you'll lose the spirit and become inactive in the Church. You'll also put your family in jeopardy."

"That will never happen to me. I have a testimony, and I'll stay active in spite of him."

Six months later the man and his entire family had left the Church.

Criticism of Church leaders damages the faith and spiritual development of children. The testimonies of most children are not well grounded in Church doctrine, and many children do not have sufficient wisdom and experience to differentiate between Church doctrine and the behavior of Church leaders. Thus, when parents ridicule, condemn, or find fault with leaders, it can be, in their children's eyes, the equivalent of criticizing Church doctrine or the Church itself. And most children's fragile testimonies cannot withstand such an attack without suffering permanent damage.

In citing research on the subject, Gene Dalton observed, "The Mormon parents, who had apparently been reared in active homes themselves, constantly complained and criticized Church authorities, but they never left the Church nor abandoned its teachings as guides in their lives. They were too much a product of their own upbringing to do so. But their children, who had heard the chafing and the criticisms at the dinner table all their lives, did leave—to the partial dismay of their parents."[10]

Rearing children is such an important yet unpredictable challenge that, to be successful, most of us need all the help we can get. We never know who will be called to teach or lead our children. So to destroy the credibility of a future leader or teacher is of such serious consequence as to hardly go unnoticed by the Almighty in the eternal scheme of things. Under such conditions, the law of the harvest often comes into play: "Whatsoever ye sow, that shall ye also reap." (D&C 6:33.)

Several years ago, a counselor in a Young Women's Presidency had a serious conflict with the Scoutmaster over the scheduling of some church facilities. Although the Scouts had previously scheduled the building, the counselor insisted that the activity for all the girls in the ward took priority. The Scoutmaster disagreed and refused to change the schedule. An appeal to the bishopric resulted in a decision in favor of the Scoutmaster.

The woman took the decision personally and singled out the Scoutmaster for being at fault. She shared her feelings with anyone who would listen. Unfortunately, her most captive audience sat around her dinner table each evening; and for two years she consistently pointed out the man's shortcomings to her four teenage children.

Two-and-one-half years after the incident, the Scoutmaster was called to serve as the bishop. At about the same time, the woman began having trouble with her oldest daughter. When the problems became quite serious, this woman, now repentant, went to her bishop for assistance. However, when he sat down with the daughter, she refused to even listen—he had absolutely no credibility with the girl. The continuous diet of criticism had rendered him powerless.

Regardless of the seriousness of our problems with others or the depth of our feelings about those problems, it is in our and our children's best interests to avoid criticism. On the other hand, supporting Church leaders helps to create an environment that encourages leaders to successfully fulfill their stewardship, thereby blessing the lives of those they serve. Children need to know that their leaders can help them; and both the children and the leaders are empowered when they have faith in each other. A former branch president shared the following incident:

> The young man was just completing his Ph.D. and was contemplating a move to another state. The problem he presented was complex. I told him that I had no idea what he should do.
>
> "I can't accept that," he said. "You're my branch president. You're entitled to receive inspiration for me. I have a serious problem, and I don't know what to do about it. When I prayed, I felt prompted to come to you for counsel."
>
> I was touched by his faith. As I bowed my head in silent prayer, the answer immediately came to me. We discussed how the solution to his problem could be implemented, and he left the meeting confident that he was on course and that the counsel he had received was inspired. His faith in the divine nature of my call made it possible for me to provide the assistance he needed.

When we teach our children to support and sustain Church leaders, we make it possible for them to draw on the important spiritual resources that leaders can provide. Inspired leaders can help only if we sustain them and listen to their counsel. Thus, a testimony that they are "called of God by prophecy" allows them to serve as instruments in the Lord's hands to bless our families.

10

Let Them Make Choices

As I walked up the front steps, I could hear someone yelling inside. I took a deep breath, rang the doorbell, clutched the fast-offering envelopes, and waited. Blair yanked open the front door with all of the strength available in his eleven-year-old frame. "What do you want?" he demanded.

"I'm here to collect fast offerings."

"Mom, Mike is here to collect fast offerings, and I'm not going."

"It's your decision," his mother said. "You don't have to go to church if you don't want to. You've been taught right from wrong. So make up your own mind." Sister Smith then looked at me, smiled, and said, "Hi. Thank you for coming. I've been expecting you." She took the check off the piano and placed it in the fast-offering envelope.

Blair continued, "I'm not going, and you can't do anything about it."

"You're right, and I don't intend to try. You can do whatever you want. I'm going to church because that's where Heavenly Father wants me to be. You have to make up your own mind."

"Why do I always have to go to church? I hate church."

She answered, "You're not being forced to go to church. It's up to you whether you go. If you don't want to go, then stay home." She handed me the fast-offering envelope, smiled, and said, "Thank you very much for coming."

"I told you that I'm not going. I want to stay home and read.

*If I have to, I'll even read the Book of Mormon. But I'm not
going to church."*

"Okay, I got the message, so you don't need to say any more.
The decision is yours. You know what your Father in Heaven
expects of you. When you were baptized, you promised him that
you would keep his commandments. You have to decide if you're
really going to do that. I'm going to church. If you want, I'll
save you a seat. But the choice is yours."

"I told you, I'm not going." Blair then threw the comics on
the living-room sofa and stomped out of the room.

As I was leaving, I asked, "What was that all about?"

"He's just trying to grow up. I hope and pray that I live
long enough to raise that boy—there's not another person on this
earth who understands him."

An hour later, as I was walking out of the ward clerk's office,
I was surprised to see Blair standing by the water fountain. "I
thought you weren't coming to church today."

Blair smiled at me, shrugged his shoulders, and said, "I
changed my mind."

Teach Children to Make Choices

The gift of agency is universal. It comes from God to everyone. Parents have the responsibility to teach their children to
exercise that gift properly by making right decisions; the quality
of their lives, both in this world and in the next, depends upon
it. To develop decision-making skills, children need practice; and
the most effective way to get that practice is to have abundant
opportunities to make choices. For most children, the choosing
process can begin very early. As one mother explained:

> I start giving my children choices as soon as they can
> understand what I'm saying. "Do you want half a glass of
> milk or all the way to the top?" "Do you want to take your
> bath right now or in a few minutes?" "Do you want plain
> water or bubble bath?" "Do you want to wear your pink
> pajamas or your blue ones?" "Do you want to wear your
> white shirt or your blue one to church today?" "Which
> bedtime story would you like me to read?" These are the
> kind of choices that I give my children before they turn

two. Between two and four years old, I expand the choices. That way I'm not constantly having to say "no." As they get older, the opportunities to choose increase.

In providing choices, however, I always make certain that I can live with whatever they decide. If they then refuse to make a decision, I will make it for them. In fact, I never give my children a choice unless I'm willing to make it for them. They want parents who are strong enough to take care of them.

Providing children with choices does not mean that they have unrestricted freedom. Clear limits need to be established, particularly as they relate to physical and spiritual health; and children need to understand exactly what those limits are. To illustrate this point, consider the following statement by a father about his son:

> As we were riding home from town the other day, my eleven-year-old son asked me to stop the car so he could run the rest of the way home. "Where are you going to run?" I asked.
>
> "Oh, up through the neighborhood."
>
> "You can run straight down this road for two miles, or you can ride the two miles with me in the car. Either one is fine with me."
>
> "I want to run through the neighborhood."
>
> "What are your choices?" I asked.
>
> "But Dad, that isn't fair."
>
> "What are your choices?"
>
> "I don't want to do either of them."
>
> I smiled at him again and said, "Son, what are your choices?"
>
> He smiled back at me and said, "I'll run down the road."

Thus, as long as our children's behavior falls within acceptable boundaries, they can be given a great deal of freedom in which to grow and develop. For example, one father said:

> When my children are little, there are areas in which they don't get to choose. We don't give them a choice about playing on the roof, or entertaining themselves with loaded

70

guns, or taking dangerous drugs. They also don't get to make choices about going to church, kneeling in family prayer, attending family home evening, or keeping the Word of Wisdom. It's not that we force them to go to church or to pray. We just do it, and they go along. The consequences of unwise decisions in those areas are simply too expensive; they are too young, and they lack the experience to make sound decisions.

Fortunately, most decisions children make don't fall into the "life and death" category. So if they make mistakes, we and they can live with them. Let them make mistakes because that's the secret of learning—making mistakes and learning from them. Remember, the duty we have as parents is to rear responsible children who are well grounded in gospel principles and who have strong testimonies, so that when they go out into the world, they can make a contribution. We want them to be assets, rather than liabilities. Children can't learn to be responsible without making mistakes. *Just keep the price affordable.*

What does *affordable* mean? Allowing them to get hit by a car while playing in the street or letting them poison themselves is something we can't afford. Going without dessert or getting into trouble with a playmate next door, however, is affordable. One good thing about children making mistakes when they're young is that their mistakes are usually inexpensive, in the sense that little damage is done, and they can easily get up and try again. An elementary-school principal explained it this way:

> A girl forgets her homework, and what's the price tag? She gets a zero in the teacher's grade book. Can she pick herself up and try again? Sure. . . . What if Karen forgets her field trip slip? She doesn't get to go. Can she pick herself up and try again, or is she a disadvantaged student from then on?
>
> What about a forgotten lunch? There we're into serious business, because there's no more emotional issue in any school in the land than a child who did not get his lunch. According to pediatricians I've consulted, there's not one documented case of a child dying between noon and 3:00 P.M. because he forgot his lunch! Also, it's interesting to

71

note that in all the years we offered vegetables and salad to students who forgot their lunches, not one kid ever took us up on it![1]

Parents sometimes overreact when their children don't adhere perfectly to gospel standards, particularly when they are younger. As long as the price is affordable, however, there is wisdom in letting the children learn from their mistakes. A prudent stepmother told us the following:

One Sunday afternoon my thirteen-year-old daughter got a call from her best friend. Several girls had pulled together a swimming party, and she wanted to go. She pleaded, "Mom, I know all the reasons why I shouldn't, but I want to do it just this once!"

"I don't think it is a wise decision, but it's up to you. You decide."

"Okay, then I'll go," she said.

Three hours later, when she returned, she was quiet and pensive. I said, "Hi. How did things go?"

She responded with an unenthusiastic, "Fine."

"Do you want to talk about it?"

"Nope."

Later that evening, as we had our usual bedtime chat, she said, "Mom, it wasn't worth it to break the Sabbath. I didn't have that much fun. I felt sort of a sick, let-down feeling. I don't think I ever want to do that again."

I said, "Honey, I'm glad you've made that decision. Heavenly Father loves us and knew what he was doing when he asked us to keep the Sabbath Day holy."

"I wish you had said I couldn't go."

"Would you have learned anything if I had done that?"

"Probably not."

Six months later she joined a volleyball team at the local recreation center. After the first practice, she learned that, due to scheduling problems, the team would have to practice on Sunday. She promptly quit the team. When the teammates pushed her for a reason, she said smilingly, "My religion teaches me that I shouldn't do things like that on Sunday, and I want to live my religion." At the dinner table that night, she said, "I learned my lesson six months ago. I'm never going to let something like that happen again."

Making decisions is an important factor in growth and development. The more children apply gospel principles to their decisions, the better they become at seeing how the gospel affects their lives. As parents, we can hope that, by the time they're teenagers, they'll have had so much experience that the first thing they think of when major decisions come along is, "What impact will this have on me?" But that doesn't mean they'll like it. As one mother cautioned:

> Don't expect to be popular with your children when you stop telling them "No." When my children come to me with a problem or a request, I try to discuss the implications and explain to them what I see as the costs. I then tell them, "I've taught you the best that I can. Now you need to make the decision. I'm sure you'll do the right thing." My son once said, "I hate that. You never tell us what to do. We always have to make up our own minds." He got the point, even though he didn't like it very well.

Even with practice, children will make mistakes. When that happens, they need a safe place to learn the important lessons that those mistakes can offer. As children get older, the stakes increase, and the cost of poor choices becomes much more expensive. One father explained that his two daughters, who graduated from high school in the late 1980s, had made more life-and-death decisions—decisions about drugs, sex, alcohol, fast cars, careers—in a week than he had in all of his high-school years. When he was in high school, he couldn't have bought hard drugs if he had wanted to, and there was no such thing as AIDS. Given the challenges children face today, it is critical that they learn how to make proper decisions.

Those youth who have had experience with making decisions understand the degree to which they control their lives; and that is a very freeing knowledge. They have learned that the quality of their decisions determines the quality of their lives. When they realize that they are in control, they often find it easier to take counsel from others, particularly their parents. A senior in high school shared the following incident:

73

One night last year I asked my parents if I could go to a canyon party. My mom said she had an uneasy feeling about it and didn't think it was wise for me to go. As always, however, she said I could go if I wanted.

My parents almost never say no to me, so when they do tell me no, I listen, because it means that they usually know something I don't. I've also learned from experience that when my mother says she has an uneasy feeling about something, I'd better pay very close attention. So I chose to stay home.

The next day I learned that there had been an auto accident and several of the kids were badly injured. Imagine the impact of that decision on my life. I will be forever grateful that I listened to my mom.

Having the freedom to choose is empowering. If given a choice between feeling powerful and powerless, people will choose feeling powerful. The parent-child relationship, unfortunately, has many dynamics built into it that cause children to feel powerless. Children, like adults, need to feel that they are in control of their lives. Generally, the more they feel in control of their own lives, the less they feel a need to rebel against their parents. Rebellion is a power struggle, whether it occurs at age two or age sixteen. The only way to win that struggle is not to play. A returned missionary described his feelings this way:

Shortly after I was ordained a teacher, I began to struggle with the notion of going on a mission. I wasn't sure that that was what I wanted to do with my life. Two years is a long time. One Sunday afternoon I defiantly asked my father, "Do I have to go on a mission?"

"No," he quietly replied. "You don't have to go. That is strictly your choice. You can stay home if you want to."

I still remember how I felt when he said that. All of a sudden I realized that I had nothing to rebel against. From that moment on, going on a mission was never an issue for me.

Often it takes very little to give children the message that they are in control of their lives. A wise father did it in the following way:

74

When Jim was a sophomore, he wanted to grow a beard. Unfortunately, the only thing he could produce was a silly-looking goatee. One day one of his female friends asked me, "How come you don't make your son shave that little beard?"

"Oh, I don't know. I guess because it makes him happy." What she didn't realize was that the goatee gave him the message that he was in control of his life. What a tiny price to pay to let him know that he was in control! Now he's more inclined to listen to me on other things. He has since said several times, "Dad understands me. He let me grow a goatee. That shows he trusts and respects me." And people listen to others whom they trust and respect.

One of the major secrets of happy parenting is understanding how to avoid power struggles with children. The terrible two's is a power issue. Teenage rebellion is a power issue. The easiest way we know of to avoid power struggles is to provide children with choices. One couple handled it this way:

My wife and I decided early in our marriage that when our children came along, we wanted to minimize the points of conflict as much as possible. I have learned that if you let the children win a hefty portion of the time, they're going to honor your requests for the things that are important to you. On the other hand, if you fight them, they're going to fight you in return. So as a result, we have tried to confine ourselves to the basic things that we can't give in on. The Word of Wisdom is one of them. Being morally clean, keeping the Sabbath Day holy, and being honest are others. Almost everything else is open. If my children want to cut their hair off and be bald, it's their choice. If they want to dye their hair purple, I could live with that. They can dress any way they want to, provided they're modest. They are free to do what they want, as long as what they do won't keep them out of the celestial kingdom.

To get a perspective from the receiving end, we interviewed this couple's oldest son, a senior in high school. He told us the following:

I realized very early that I was in control of my life. I

also learned that the kinds of choices I made determined the quality of my life. My parents taught me that I have complete control over my actions, but I have no control over the consequences of those actions. I can choose how I feel. If I want to be angry, I have that freedom. If I want to be happy, I can do that too. I've watched people who live the gospel, and I've watched people who don't. I learned that those who live the gospel are much happier than the rest. People who make good decisions are happier than those who don't. Since I want to have as great a life as possible, I try to think in terms of the long run, particularly on gospel related matters.

People have asked me why I don't rebel. They don't understand. I don't have anything to rebel against. I have the freedom to choose, and my folks will still love me if I make mistakes. How do I know that? Because I have made mistakes, and they still love me. So it's hard for me to identify with kids who are trying to find themselves. I know who I am. I am a son of God, and I have the freedom to choose how I want to live my life. I have chosen to live a good life. That means that I follow the teachings of Christ. It's really very simple.

Obviously, rearing great children is more than merely providing them with choices. There has to be a lot of love, a lot of effective teaching, and a lot of praying. Life, however, is full of decisions; and the quality of our lives depends upon the quality of our decisions. Therefore, the more experience children have in making choices when the price tags are affordable, the better they will be in making good choices when they start facing the life-and-death decisions.

TOOLS
FOR TEACHING
THE GOSPEL
IN THE HOME

11

The Power of Prayer

As I leaned over the bed to kiss Matthew good night, I suddenly felt a sick feeling come over me. I immediately ran downstairs and said to my husband, "Honey, where's Rebecca?" He turned pale and said, "Good heavens! We left her at the church."

Our two oldest sons had played in a basketball game earlier that night. At 9:30 P.M. we piled seven of our eight children in the van and drove home. Not until I had put our two youngest children to bed a few minutes later did I realize that our six-year-old daughter and her girlfriend weren't with us. On the way back to the church, my husband said, "From now on I'm going to be much more understanding of Joseph and Mary for leaving Jesus in Jerusalem."

When we arrived at the church house, we found the lights off and the doors locked. We fully expected the children to be inside, but a search of the building proved otherwise. By that time I was in a state of panic.

As we walked out of the building, I saw Rebecca and her friend running across the parking lot toward us. I had never been so happy to see that little girl in my life. I hugged her so hard I thought she'd break.

On the way home Rebecca told us what had happened. Once she realized we had gone, she and her friend started to walk home. As they were crossing a park near the church, our daughter asked her friend to kneel down with her and pray. Rebecca said, "I told Heavenly Father that we were cold, all alone, and really scared, *and I asked him to help us get home safely. As soon as I finished praying, something told me to go back to the church and wait, so we came back. I was so glad to see our van that I started to cry and came running." Thankfully somewhere along the way, my little girl had learned the importance of prayer and was convinced that she could rely on her Father in Heaven for help. Childlike faith is a powerful force for good in the world.*

Teaching Children to Pray

Prayers are sacred experiences that provide opportunities to communicate with God and to pour out the righteous desires of our hearts. Since gaining a testimony without prayer is impossible, we have a sacred responsibility to teach our children how to pray, both publicly and privately.

Public prayers are offered in public settings. These prayers are formal, such as the opening and closing prayers in a worship service, when we speak for a congregation. Such prayers should be specific and relate to the needs of the people attending the meeting. They should also be kept short: "Two minutes will open any kind of meeting, and a half minute will close it."[1]

Private prayers, on the other hand, include family prayers, blessings on the food, and our secret prayers. Family prayers and private prayers are much more personal and can last longer—private prayers can be as long as we choose. Most of the instruction we receive in the scriptures relates to these secret prayers. Throughout the scriptures the Lord counsels us to pray continuously. Nothing in the gospel is better designed to keep our attention on God, on righteousness, and on fulfilling our covenants and obligations than prayer.[2]

Great blessings pour into the lives of children who learn to pray. Parents who teach their children to pray have unique opportunities to teach gospel principles and to implant in young hearts a desire to receive the blessings the Lord has in store. As a father of seven explained:

> Every night and morning, as I was growing up, I knelt at my mother's knee and asked my Heavenly Father to help me be worthy to go on a mission and to be married in the temple. Between the time I turned two and the time I was

ordained a deacon, I had asked the Lord for that blessing over seven thousand times. As a result, there was no way I would stay home and not serve a mission. Similarly, there was no way I would get married anywhere but in the temple. That desire had been implanted in me when I was little, and I wanted to live worthy of that great blessing.

When children are taught that God is a kind and loving Father who desires to bless them, they are also taught that they can freely discuss their problems and concerns with him. Under such conditions, parents can learn a great deal about the problems that face their children by listening carefully to their prayers. For instance, a young mother said:

> One night I knelt beside our seven-year-old son as he began his evening prayers. About halfway through he said, "Heavenly Father, please help me with my times tables, 'cause I'm really scared." He then broke into tears. After he calmed down, he told me that he had fallen behind the rest of his second-grade class in learning his times tables. He was upset and embarrassed to the point that he didn't want to go to school anymore. And this kid loved school.
>
> I was stunned. Neither my husband nor I had any idea that he had a problem with arithmetic. We began working with him, and within three weeks he had caught up with the rest of the class. That experience taught me an important lesson. Since that time I have paid careful attention to what my children say when they talk to their Father in Heaven.

It is one thing to teach children the mechanics of prayer, and quite another to teach them that Heavenly Father hears their prayers and will answer them in the way that is for their best good. Children who understand that their Father in Heaven loves them also understand that they can rely on him for help in the everyday difficulties of life. They develop the kind of faith that makes prayer so powerful. A father of four children shared the following experience:

> I had driven all day to get to Targhee National Park at the base of Wyoming's Teton Mountains, where my family had been camping for several days. As I got out of the car,

my eleven-year-old daughter greeted me excitedly, "Daddy, it really works. We were in trouble, and Heavenly Father answered our prayers. Heather (her cousin) and I were hiking up in the mountains. We took the wrong trail, and after about an hour we were out in the middle of nowhere, and we didn't have a clue about where we were. We knelt down, and I asked Heavenly Father if we were on the right trail. At first I didn't feel anything, but after a few seconds, I knew we were on the wrong trail and that we should go back as quickly as we could. So we ran all the way back, and Heavenly Father helped us get home safely."

"Heavenly Father really loves you," I said.

"Yeah, he really does, Daddy. I know that."

Sometimes, however, prayers don't always get answered so quickly, particularly when they relate to gaining a testimony of the gospel. For most people, the process of gaining a testimony is gradual and extends over a period of years. This is even true for prophets. Note, for example, President David O. McKay's experience:

> One day in my youth I was hunting cattle. While climbing a steep hill, I stopped to let my horse rest, and there, once again, an intense desire came over me to receive a manifestation of the truth of the restored gospel. I dismounted, threw my reins over my horse's head, and there under a serviceberry bush I prayed that God would declare to me the truth of his revelation to Joseph Smith. I am sure that I prayed fervently and sincerely and with as much faith as a young boy could muster.
>
> At the conclusion of the prayer, I arose from my knees, threw the reins over my faithful pony's head, and got into the saddle. As I started along the trail again, I remember saying to myself: "No spiritual manifestation has come to me. If I am true to myself, I must say I am just the same 'old boy' that I was before I prayed."
>
> The Lord did not see fit to give me an answer on that occasion, but in 1899, after I had been appointed president of the Scottish Conference, the spiritual manifestation for

which I had prayed as a boy in my teens came as a natural sequence to the performance of duty.[3]

There are also times when the answer we seek is not consistent with the mind and will of the Lord. Thus, children, as well as their parents, must be willing to take *no* for an answer, knowing that a wise Heavenly Father will do what is best for them. That is not always easy, particularly when the lives of loved ones hang in the balance. In recalling one of the greatest tragedies of his life, a man said:

> As long as I live, I will remember sitting on the front row of the Garland Tabernacle, with my grandmother on one side, and my seven-year-old sister on the other, looking over my mother's white velvet casket at Bishop J. Roscoe Hunt, who was speaking from the pulpit. I had turned fourteen three months earlier. My three younger sisters were ten, seven, and three. The previous six days had been the worst of my life. I felt like my entire world had fallen apart. I had prayed, as I had never prayed in my life, that my mother's life would be spared. But she died.
>
> Bishop Hunt said, "Sometimes we don't understand why the Lord doesn't answer our prayers the way we want them answered. A father had two daughters. One was married to a farmer, and the other to a potter. The wife of the farmer prayed, 'Father, please bless us with more rain, that our crops may grow.' The wife of the potter prayed, 'Father, please bless us with more dry weather, that we may have more clay for our pots.' "
>
> I remember nothing else from that sermon. But to this day I can remember the words that came into my mind: "I could not give you that for which you prayed. Someday, you will understand. But you can be at peace, knowing that I have taken your mother for a righteous purpose. She is still your mother. She loves you, and she will remain very close to you."
>
> The rest of the day is a blur. We went to the cemetery for the dedication of the grave. Later we went back to put flowers on the grave. I remember crying as though my heart would break. That night, as we knelt in family prayer, my

father thanked the Lord that we still had each other and prayed for strength. As he spoke, I again heard in my mind the sacred words that I had heard earlier in the funeral. I realized that heaven isn't very far away, and I am grateful to this day that a kind and loving Father in Heaven saw fit to comfort his heartbroken son at a time of such desperate need.

Family Prayer

Great spiritual strength is poured into families when they kneel together in family prayer. Such is the promised result of obeying the Lord's commandment to "pray in your families unto the Father, always in my name, that your wives and your children may be blessed." (3 Ne. 18:21.) By doing so, we effectively teach our children to pray. One father put it this way:

When I was growing up, I belonged to a praying family. My mother knelt with us night and morning and taught us to pray. We also prayed as a family several times a day. For example, we knelt in family prayer each morning before breakfast, and then we sat at the table and had a blessing on the food. At lunch we also blessed the food. In the evening, we knelt again as a family in family prayer, and then we sat at the table and blessed the food again. The genius of that pattern is that it provides an opportunity for more people to pray. It also focuses the family members' attention on the purposes of prayer. Family prayers were particularly significant. We learned how to talk to Heavenly Father by listening to our parents. There was a sacred, spiritual feeling in our home when we knelt in prayer together, each person taking his or her turn.

Family prayer can serve a variety of different functions. For example, consider the experience of Elder Loren C. Dunn:

No matter how tired [Dad] and Mother must have been, they never went to sleep until we were in. When I was the only one left at home, he was in the habit of not holding family prayer until I came home, even though he and Mother would be in bed. In situations like that he always called on me to pray. I want to tell you that that had quite an impact on how I conducted myself as a youth, when I knew that I was going to have to end my evening at the bedside of my parents in prayer.[4]

Family members who regularly invite the Spirit of the Lord into their homes through family prayer grow in love, loyalty, unity, and spirituality. Family prayer provides a spiritual anchor against life's trials. President Spencer W. Kimball promised parents who kneel together with their families in prayer each morning and night that their "children will learn to honor and revere the Lord's anointed leaders as they are taught to pray for their local and general authorities; they will love the Lord as they pray for his work; they will love their fellowmen as they pray for the sick, the mourners, the distressed. They will anticipate with gladness their own missions as they pray for the missionaries out preaching the gospel."[5]

Parents who kneel before the Lord and pray for their children help them to develop spiritual strength and self-confidence in ways that may otherwise be impossible. A young mother shared the following:

When we knelt together as a family, there was no question in my mind that my parents loved me. I could tell by the way they prayed. They consistently thanked Heavenly Father for us, told him how much they loved us, and explained how proud they were of the lives we were living and the choices we were making. They also asked him to bless each of us in the areas we needed the most. We grew up thinking we were the most important children in the world, and we did all we could to live up to the way they described us when they spoke about us to the Lord.

Regular family prayer also provides opportunities for children to have profound spiritual experiences. Few activities reveal the character of family members quite so much as their kneeling before the Lord and pouring out their souls to Heavenly Father. On such occasions the Holy Ghost descends upon families and strengthens all who are present. Recalling a tender memory years later, a priesthood holder told this story:

When I was a boy, my dad and I went to the Vernal,

Utah, area each fall to get our firewood for the winter. We always stayed with my grandparents. One of the great blessings of those trips was the privilege of hearing my grandfather pray. When I was fourteen, I took a friend along. On the way home from that trip, my friend said to my dad, "When we knelt down in family prayer this morning, and David's grandfather was praying, I actually thought Jesus was there in the room. In fact, I wanted to open my eyes and see him!" I knew exactly what he was talking about, because I had experienced those same feelings several times.

Will any other activity have a more unifying impact upon our families than consistently kneeling together each morning and evening in family prayer? Children who participate in praying as a family have ingrained in their hearts and minds a deep, abiding love for their Father in Heaven.

12

Developing a Love
for the Scriptures

The color immediately left Danny's face, and I heard a sick-
ening groan. He grabbed his stomach with both hands, gasped
for breath, and fell to the living-room floor. After what seemed
like an eternity, he started to cry. Taylor, his older brother by
two years, stood over him with both fists doubled up, glaring at
his eleven-year-old sibling. "That's just a taste of what you're
going to get the next time you make fun of the way I read."

Now I am not so naive as to expect things to go perfectly all
of the time. But this wasn't supposed to happen. Reading the
scriptures is supposed to be a spiritual experience. The prophet
said so. But my children hate it. They don't pay attention. They
make fun of each other. And now we have a full-blown fist fight,
right in the middle of Helaman 12. There has got to be a better
way!

Blessings That Come from Reading the Scriptures

Scripture study is an important key to understanding the
principles and ordinances of the gospel, and it is absolutely
essential to the process of gaining a testimony. The scriptures
contain God's teachings to mankind, and their importance cannot be overstated. When the Lord commanded Nephi to slay
Laban in order to obtain the brass plates, he explained, "It is
better that one man should perish than that a nation should
dwindle and perish in unbelief." (1 Ne. 4:13.)

The Lord expects us to understand the scriptures. Jesus commanded his disciples, "Search the scriptures; for in them ye think ye have eternal life: and they are they which testify of me." (John 5:39.) President Ezra Taft Benson strongly counseled the Saints about the importance of scriptural study and encouraged Church members to immerse themselves in the scriptures, explaining that "when individual members and families immerse themselves in the scriptures regularly and consistently, these other areas of activity will automatically come. Testimonies will increase. Commitment will be strengthened. Families will be fortified. Personal revelation will flow."[1]

Thus, teaching our children to study and cherish the scriptures is vital. The word of God has been preserved by the power of God to provide us with the gospel truths. Great blessings come to those who regularly read the scriptures. As a single mother of four explained:

> Five years ago I sat in stake conference and heard our stake president plead with the members to read the Book of Mormon each day. He then shared the following statement by President Marion G. Romney:
>
> "I counsel you . . . everywhere, to make reading in the Book of Mormon a few minutes each day a lifelong practice. . . . I feel certain that if, in our homes, parents will read from the Book of Mormon prayerfully and regularly, both by themselves and with their children, the spirit of that great book will come to permeate our homes and all who dwell therein. The spirit of reverence will increase, mutual respect and consideration for each other will grow. The spirit of contention will depart. Parents will counsel their children in greater love and wisdom. Children will be more responsive and submissive to that counsel. Righteousness will increase. Faith, hope, and charity—the pure love of Christ—will abound in our homes and lives, bringing in their wake peace, joy, and happiness."[2]
>
> I have four sons, three of whom were teenagers at the time, and I desperately needed the blessings President Romney promised. Since 6:00 A.M. was the only time we could regularly be together as a family, we agreed to read the Book of Mormon for ten minutes each morning before sem-

inary. So every night, when I set the table for the next day's breakfast, I placed a copy of the scriptures by each plate, just so we wouldn't forget.

I can bear testimony of the truthfulness of President Romney's words. The Holy Ghost came into our family as we had never experienced. The boys became more respectful and considerate. The contention left. I became more effective in helping my sons, and they responded more positively to my counsel. All four of my sons grew to love the Book of Mormon, and the three who are old enough have served missions. Every blessing that President Romney promised has been fulfilled in our family. What I thought would be a burden turned out to be a source of joy.

President Benson explained that studying the scriptures is not a burden laid upon us by the Lord. Rather, it is a marvelous opportunity:

> If we ignore what the Lord has given us, we may lose the very power and blessings which we seek. . . . Let us not treat lightly the great things we have received from the Lord! His word is one of the most valuable gifts He has given us. I urge you to recommit yourselves to a study of the scriptures. Immerse yourselves in them daily so you will have the power of the Spirit to attend you in your callings. Read them in your families and teach your children to love and treasure them.[3]

Ideas for Reading the Scriptures

Carefully studying the scriptures daily is an invaluable tool for teaching children the gospel. If we want our children to gain testimonies, we must read the scriptures ourselves and then instill within our children a love for the teachings of the prophets. The challenge comes in knowing how to effectively teach our children to love the scriptures. Knowing what is important is one thing. Doing it in a way that is both enjoyable and instructional is entirely different. Granted, it is not an easy task; and in order to accomplish it, families must dedicate themselves to developing the habit of scripture study. A father described the method he and his wife used to motivate his three children to study the scriptures:

We decided that if scripture study was going to work in my family, we had to establish a habit of reading every day. No exceptions. We called a family council, and we set a goal to read the scriptures each day. It didn't matter what we read, where we read, or how much we read, as long as we read the scriptures. We kept track of our progress, and at the end of each week we celebrated our success. This gave us the motivation to both get started and to keep it going until it became a habit. Our approach worked remarkably well, and soon the scriptures became an essential part of our lives.

As the children grew older, we expanded the goal of a week at a time to two weeks, to a month, and then to three months. Soon, the celebration became unimportant. We had learned to love the scriptures. Our knowledge of the scriptures improved, and our spirituality increased. We started having family prayer and regular family home evening. We also felt much closer to God. Family unity and harmony increased, and we found ourselves better able to work out family problems.

Something else happened that surprised me. During family discussions, the children began to use stories from the scriptures to illustrate their points. They also began asking more questions, some of which surprised me. For example, within the past month my nine-year-old son asked the following questions:

• What is it like to be in hell?
• How could Mary be a virgin if she had a baby?
• What did Jesus mean when he said, "I and my Father are one?"
• If Christ went to heaven when he died, why did he tell Mary not to touch him because he had not ascended to his Father?

Questions like these frequently provide an excuse for extensive gospel discussions. Before we started reading the scriptures, such things had never happened in our family — and all this has come because we developed a habit of reading only a few verses each day. There is great truth in the statement, "Out of small things proceedeth that which is great." (D&C 64:33.)

Reading the scriptures aloud can help children become comfortable with the language of the scriptures. That's why reading the scriptures to them when they are very young is so important. As one man explained:

> I used to listen to my father read the scriptures to us every day before breakfast. I can still hear him reading to me the parable of the prodigal son. My father was accidentally killed when I was nine years old, but I had heard him read the scriptures for three or four years and those passages are still in my mind. That was the most important part of my education. . . .
>
> As children [we] learned language mainly by hearing it constantly about us in contexts that enabled us to understand it. Our children, hearing the scriptures day by day and absorbing them from the very beginning of their lives, will be at home with the language of the scriptures. No other way of learning to read the scriptures is as good. So, it is our duty to read the scriptures aloud daily with our children, no matter what age they may be. If we do not, they will never learn to read the scriptures half so well by themselves.[4]

Children may or may not fully understand the doctrine, but by learning the language of the scriptures as they grow, they become familiar with the scriptures and develop a love for them. A father of five girls described his experience this way:

> When our oldest child was eight months old, she got the croup and couldn't sleep at night. The only things that calmed her down were for me to rock her and to talk to her. I was taking a Book of Mormon class at the time, and I had to do my homework. So for several months I read the scriptures to her each night. I am not certain of the extent to which that had an impact on her, but to this day she dearly loves the scriptures; and I attribute that love to the fact that they were read to her so much during her first year.

Most families find it difficult to develop the daily habit of reading the scriptures together. Busy activities and different ages often deter regular family scripture study. Fortunately, the schedule doesn't seem to matter as long as it fits the needs of the family. Some families get up fifteen minutes early and read before the normal day gets started. Others read together before, during, or after the evening meal. Still others read before the youngest children go to bed. Consider the following comments from a single mother of six:

> Since I am divorced and work full time, reading scriptures with the children has been a special challenge. For a few weeks after President Benson asked us to read the Book of Mormon each day, we experimented with different ways to do it. We read in the morning before school, and we read at the dinner table. Sometimes we were successful. Most of the time we weren't. It seemed like an impossible task, and since there was never a time when the whole family could be together, we quit. I knew the decision was not right, but I'm willing to fight only so many battles, and that wasn't one of them.
>
> Then while attending a wedding in another state, we spent the night with some close friends. At bedtime the father asked, "Would you like to join us for scripture reading?" Everyone had his or her own copy of the Book of Mormon, and we went around the room with each person reading one verse.
>
> At first I thought it was a bit strange, because the family members weren't all present like they were supposed to be. However, it didn't matter if their oldest son had not yet returned home; they still read the scriptures. After we finished the chapter, we knelt in family prayer. The father and mother then hugged and kissed their children, and it was over. The whole thing hadn't taken more than twenty minutes.
>
> I thought, "Bedtime is the answer — and everyone doesn't have to be there." That thought had never occurred to me before. We started as soon as I got home.
>
> Now, when the first person gets ready for bed, we stop

whatever we're doing, and those who are home gather together in the living room. The person to my left reads the first verse, and we proceed in turn around the room. We don't always read a complete chapter. With my children, the attention span is short, so we go around the room only four times. There are seven of us, so when all of us are home, we read twenty-eight verses. Sometimes we discuss what we read. Sometimes we don't. After family prayer, everyone goes on about their business.

This schedule may not work for everyone, but it has certainly worked for us. We've been doing it for six months now, and we have missed only one or two nights. My children are developing a love for the scriptures that I never thought possible, and we have had some wonderful, tender experiences. It has created opportunities for us to talk about the gospel and things that are important to us, in ways that we had never before experienced. I've felt the Spirit much more in our home since we began reading the scriptures. The surprising thing for me is that it is so simple. I don't know why it didn't occur to me before.

There are also variations in how much time families spend reading the scriptures and in how they read them. Some families read one chapter a day. Others read for fifteen minutes. One family has a jar filled with scriptural verses. Each evening at the dinner table, a child takes one slip of paper from the jar and reads it to the family; they then discuss that topic during dinner and determine how it applies to their lives.

Since there is not an "only way" to successfully read the scriptures, most families experiment a bit before they discover what works for them. But one thing is clear: God has promised us that regular scripture study will powerfully affect the lives of family members, and when we prayerfully consider the scriptures, he will bless us with the wisdom to make right choices for our families. For example, a father of four described his experience in this way:

My wife and I thoroughly enjoy reading the scriptures together. We typically start at the beginning of the book and plow through to the end. However, that approach never really excited my children. They read with us, and they enjoyed reading, but it didn't excite them as we had hoped. After fasting and prayer, we felt impressed to make a list of our favorite stories from the scriptures. Our four children each selected their five favorites, and my wife and I added passages we thought important. Each evening, after dinner but just before dessert, we take turns choosing the one we want to read. The children love it. It's fun for them, so there's no resistance whatsoever.

Before we started this, the younger ones never really understood what was going on. But now they look forward to scripture time, and they get excited when they can choose their scripture and everyone else in the family participates.

All four children have developed a love for the scriptures, and in the process they are building a solid foundation of gospel principles. Our original pool of thirty stories has since expanded to seventy stories and doctrinal passages. Typically, the children add the stories; my wife and I add the rest. We have found that the children have become intimately familiar with major sections of the four Standard Works.

One Sunday in sacrament meeting, as someone was giving a talk, my seven-year-old daughter whispered to me, "That's a famous passage right there." The only reason that passage was famous was because it was one of "our" scriptures.

In selecting stories, considering the needs of the children is important. Dennis and Sandra Packard describe their experience in the following way:"

These days, we're choosing fairly short passages of scripture, passages a minute or two long. When our children are older and their sense of continuity is stronger, we'll no doubt choose longer ones, maybe a whole book, like the book of Mosiah, reading a portion each night. We'll continue, of course, letting our children take turns choosing. And for now, we are doing all the reading. As soon as they're able, we'll let them take turns doing that, too.

We keep several things in mind as we choose what to

read. We select passages we particularly like, ones that say something to us. We look for passages we can give easily remembered names to, often stories and sometimes passages on particular topics, especially those topics we want our children to learn about at their ages. We pick stories that have elements children enjoy, such as animals, children, and repetition.[5]

There are many ways to successfully read the scriptures as a family, and flexibility is a key in meeting the changing needs of family members: if one approach doesn't work, try something else. The important thing is to make scripture reading an enjoyable experience for everyone involved. When that happens, the Spirit is unrestrained, and those present will have great experiences. Such was not always the case in a family with nine children. As the father explained:

As far back as I can remember, scripture reading has been a battle ground. Our pattern was to go around the room, each person reading two verses. But the children wouldn't follow along. I always caught somebody horsing around between turns. We often had quarreling. The children criticized and laughed at each other when they mispronounced words. They also yelled at one another if they read an extra verse. Sometimes they even slugged each other. It was awful.

Three years ago a friend of mine said, "You're killing yourself. Get the scriptures on audiotape – it'll make all the difference in the world." So I bought a set.

The next morning I said to the family, "Okay now, we're no longer going to read two verses each, and listen to the big children make fun of the little children because they can't pronounce the words. Everybody will just listen to this professional recording."

I turned on the tape recorder, and to my amazement, we had dead silence the entire time. The children followed along in their own books. There was no horsing around. Nobody got slugged. Nobody made fun of anybody. It was wonderful.

Scripture reading has since become an enjoyable experience. Each morning at 6:30 I make a pass through the house and announce that it's time to read the scriptures. I then go into the living room, wait for about sixty seconds, and then turn on the tape recorder. Most of the time the children are ready to begin. Sometimes a few of them are scrambling, trying to finish getting dressed. But the hassling has stopped.

The spirit of our scripture study has completely changed. We're able to go twice as fast: the speaker on the tape moves quickly, and we read a chapter every morning. The younger ones are able to follow along, and it helps them learn words without mispronouncing them.

The conflict has completely stopped. There's never a mispronounced word. There's no criticizing. The children no longer pound on each other. It is wonderful.

The tapes also allow us to have flexibility without offending the reader. If we come to something important, I'll stop the recorder and ask, "What does this mean? What's going on here?" Then we take a few minutes to talk about them. I resume the recording, and the person on tape doesn't even realize we stopped.

Once we finish our chapter, we kneel in family prayer. Almost without exception the person praying thanks Heavenly Father for the scriptures and for the Spirit we have felt. When my children leave home, they know that they started their day right because we read the scriptures. It's been a significant way to formally teach the gospel in our home.

Regardless of the reading schedule, or the variations in how a family reads the scriptures, the Lord will pour out the Spirit upon them, and family members will gain a love for the scriptures. Bishop J. Richard Clarke shared the following experience about this principle:

> I am convinced that families, even young children, can learn to love the scriptures. A few years ago when I was in Colorado Springs for a conference, I called on Mark McConkie, son of Elder and Sister Bruce R. McConkie, to address the question "How did you develop a love for the scriptures?"

As I recall, he said: "I first developed a love for the scriptures from my mother. I remember she would teach me while she did her ironing. I felt how she loved the scriptures by the way she would speak about the prophets. How much she loved them! As I grew older, I would listen to the recordings of the scriptures. I wanted to know the scriptures like my father. Sometimes he would enter the room while I was listening and it would take him just a moment to identify the exact scripture I was listening to. I wanted to be able to do that."[6]

Under such conditions, family members learn to love the scriptures, and they, like Nephi of old, can say with conviction: "My soul delighteth in the scriptures, and my heart pondereth them, and writeth them for the learning and the profit of my children. Behold, my soul delighteth in the things of the Lord." (2 Ne. 4:15–16.)

13

Attendance at Church Meetings

I was sick and tired of hearing about it. As the mother of five children, I had an ongoing battle with my children about attending church meetings. I heard constant complaints about unprepared teachers, boring speakers, hot meetings, and unfriendly peers. They said they weren't learning anything; and since learning the gospel and partaking of the sacrament were the reasons they went to church, I was hard pressed to justify why I made them suffer so much each Sunday.

Then one Sunday evening, while reading Faith Precedes the Miracle, *I came across the following statement by President Spencer W. Kimball:*

> *We do not go to Sabbath meetings to be entertained or even simply to be instructed.* We *go to worship the Lord. It is an individual responsibility, and regardless of what is said from the pulpit, if one wishes to worship the Lord in spirit and in truth, he may do so by attending his meetings, partaking of the sacrament, and contemplating the beauties of the gospel. If the service is a failure to you, you have failed. No one can worship for you; you must do your own waiting upon the Lord.[1]*

Our family home evening lesson the next night was on the keeping the Sabbath day holy. I read President Kimball's statement, and we then spent the next hour and a half discussing church meetings, selfishness, and the meaning of worshiping the Lord. I explained to the children that they weren't forced to attend

98

church, just as they weren't forced to pray or to keep any of God's other commandments. They had their agency to make their own choices.

Once our children learned that they go to church to worship the Lord and that the responsibility fell squarely on them and nobody else, the problem was resolved. Since that time we have had no problem with church attendance. The children are now doing the right thing for the right reason.

The Importance of Church Meetings

Spiritual growth comes from activity in the Church; and by definition, being active in the Church is impossible without attending church meetings. The Lord expects his children to keep the Sabbath day holy, and that includes attending the designated meetings. The sick and afflicted might have an excuse. The rest of us do not. Substituting scripture study at home is not an alternative to church attendance.

In order for children to gain testimonies of the gospel, the Holy Ghost must bear witness to them that the gospel is true. The best way to have spiritual experiences is to go to those places where the Spirit of the Lord is present. Thus, church meetings and activities provide rich opportunities for spiritual growth. As the Lord promised, "For where two or three are gathered together in my name, there am I in the midst of them." (Matt. 18:20.) The purpose of the gospel is to build people, to exalt them, and to help them return to and live with their Heavenly Father. The programs of the Church are designed to accomplish that task. As one father explained,

> My brother became the principal of a high school where the children never went to class; they spent their time out in the halls. He immediately changed the school's grading policy; a major part of the grade was based on attendance. His basic philosophy: If the children aren't in class, they don't get the benefits from going to school.
>
> I have a similar philosophy about church attendance. The Lord has asked us to attend church meetings so he can bless us. We are taught gospel principles by dedicated teachers in an environment conducive to feeling the spirit of the

Lord. We associate with great people of all ages. We partake of the sacrament and renew the covenants we made when we were baptized; and in the process, we learn the importance of keeping covenants. We find out who we are and what God expects us to be. We worship the Lord. These are all blessings that come from attending Church.

Parents need to take the initiative to help their children develop the habit of attending meetings. President Kimball explained the impact of his early Church attendance: "When I was a small boy, I was taught the habit of going to sacrament meetings. Mother always took me with her. Those warm afternoons I soon became drowsy and leaned over on her lap to sleep. I may not have learned much from the sermons, but I learned the habit of 'going to meeting.' The habit stayed with me through my life."[2]

A mother of five children under the age of twelve explained her attitude toward Church attendance as follows: "In our home, going to church is not up for negotiation. None of our children are old enough to make that kind of decision. The Lord commanded me not to let my children "transgress the laws of God." (Mosiah 4:14.) Keeping the Sabbath day holy is one of God's laws. They must attend their church meetings to obey that commandment. I try to make it as pleasant as possible for them. But in our house, we go to church. It's just part of being a member of this family."

The Lord has designed the Church programs to help us grow spiritually. Of course, it is impossible to predict when important spiritual experiences will take place in our children's lives. One thing, however, is certain: if our children don't attend the meetings where those spiritual experiences take place, they won't get the blessings. When they do attend, they sometimes have experiences that profoundly affect their lives. Consider what this fourteen-year-old girl would have missed had she not chosen to keep the Sabbath day holy and attend her church meetings. Her father described the situation this way:

> Our children have always considered stake conference synonymous with cruel and unusual punishment. They go

because they have to. After all, two hours of conference meetings once every six months is not too big a sacrifice, particularly in light of the other blessings that membership in the Church provides. Besides, attending church is simply expected in our family.

Unfortunately, our fourteen-year-old daughter has found stake conference particularly distasteful, and yesterday, before we left for the meeting, she announced that she would rather go to the dentist; and she hates going to the dentist.

We arrived early and planted ourselves on the second row, directly in front of the pulpit. As we waited for the services to begin, I suggested that she ask her Heavenly Father to help her feel good about being there and to understand the message that he had for her. Privately, I pled with the Lord to bless her with a spiritual experience.

During the first hour nothing unusual happened. Although the speeches were not boring, I also would not call them outstanding. However, she listened intently.

As we stood to sing the "rest hymn," something wonderful happened. The organist began to play hymn #134, "I Believe in Christ," and I immediately felt an outpouring of the Spirit of the Lord. By the time we began the second verse, I was so choked up, I couldn't sing. My wife was sobbing. My daughter, however, sang enthusiastically.

Later, as she helped my wife prepare Sunday dinner, she said, "Today is the first time I've ever listened to the speakers in stake conference. When we sang that song, I had the most wonderful feeling I've ever had. I almost shook, and I felt as if I had the chills. I know that the gospel is true. I know that Jesus died for us. My Heavenly Father let me know that today while we were singing. I don't understand why anyone would want to take drugs when they could have that kind of experience. You know, the only thing I feel bad about is that Susan [her best friend] wasn't there to feel what I felt. It would have been really helpful to her; but she decided to stay home because stake conference is boring."

When we attend church meetings, the Lord gives us blessings that we can get in no other way. And occasionally, those opportunities come once in a lifetime, as illustrated by the following example:

At 7:00 P.M. on October 10, 1958, the Aaronic Priesthood Memorial Monument was dedicated on Temple Square in Salt Lake City. President David O. McKay conducted the services and offered the dedicatory prayer. There was not an empty seat in the Tabernacle, and the overflow crowd filled the Assembly Hall to capacity.

A combined Aaronic Priesthood chorus from the Salt Lake Valley provided the music for the dedicatory service. I was one of four young men who represented our ward in that chorus. In addition to participating in the opening hymn, "We Thank Thee, O God, for a Prophet," we sang three other hymns that evening: "Priesthood of God," "Priesthood Song of Triumph," and "The Spirit of God like a Fire Is Burning."

After each member of the Presiding Bishopric had spoken, we sang our second song: "Priesthood of God." The choir sang the first verse and the chorus. A young man, whom I shall call Tom, had been asked to sing the second verse as a solo. He was a first tenor. When I heard him sing during our practices, I marveled at the beauty and clarity of his voice and at the composed and confident way he handled himself. Clearly few, if any, young men in the Church could have done as well.

During his solo, Tom faced the audience as he stood on a platform directly behind the First Presidency: President David O. McKay, President Stephen L Richards, and President J. Reuben Clark, Jr.

After we finished the first verse, Tom began. He sang beautifully: "We honor the glorious priesthood; 'tis a gift from the Lord in our day. With our faith firm and secure, and a love that will endure, we are called in God's appointed way." Then something terrible happened. The organ continued to play, but Tom stopped singing. He had forgotten the words.

Awkwardly, he fumbled through his note cards, but he could neither find his place nor regain his composure. It seemed an eternity before the choir joined him in the chorus and the final verse of that hymn.

I still remember the terrible feeling I had in the pit of my stomach. I became sick to my stomach, and I actually wept for him because of the pain he must have felt.

Immediately after we finished singing, President McKay stood up to conduct the remainder of the service. Before that time, I had felt few positive feelings for President McKay. I wasn't even sure that I had a testimony that he was a prophet. I had heard him speak on the radio and had seen him conduct general conference on television; but I had never seen him in person. I really didn't know what to expect, except that I was excited and honored with the opportunity to participate in that great event.

What I experienced that night, in that one single meeting, changed my life. I shall never forget what President McKay said on that occasion and how he handled that situation. As nearly as I can remember, he said:

"When I was a young boy in Huntsville, Utah, I was thrilled with the opportunity to be ordained a priest. The following Sunday I was assigned to bless the bread at the sacrament table. In those days, we were not allowed to read the prayers from a card, like you young men do today. We had to have the prayer memorized, word for word. I still remember practicing that prayer over and over in the attic of our home during the week prior to my first assignment.

"To ensure that we said the prayers correctly, each Sunday my father, who was the bishop of our ward, would lean over the pulpit that stood directly above the sacrament table and listen carefully to make sure that the priests offered the sacrament prayers correctly.

"As I knelt there at the sacrament table, I began to pray: 'O God, the Eternal Father, we ask thee in the name of thy Son, Jesus Christ, to bless and sanctify this bread to the souls of all those who partake of it. Amen.'

"My father said, 'that they may eat in remembrance of the body of thy Son'; and I said, 'that they may eat in remembrance of the body of thy Son. Amen.'

"My father then said, 'and witness unto thee, O God,

the Eternal Father'; and I said, 'and witness unto thee, O God, the Eternal Father. Amen.'

"My father then said, 'that they are willing to take upon them the name of thy Son'; and I said, 'that they are willing to take upon them the name of thy Son. Amen.'

"My father added, 'and always remember him and keep his commandments which he has given them'; and I said, 'and always remember him and keep his commandments which he has given them. Amen.'

"My father then said, 'that they may always have his Spirit to be with them'; and I said, 'that they may always have his Spirit to be with them. Amen.' "

President McKay then went on to conduct the remainder of the dedicatory service. Not a word was said about Tom. But every Aaronic Priesthood holder and leader in that audience got a clear, simple message from a prophet of God: "Everyone makes mistakes, even prophets. So don't worry anymore about this one." From that moment on, I loved President David O. McKay with all my heart.

I heard President McKay speak many times after that. I have seven of his books in my library at home, and I have read them all. But never have I been so profoundly taught what it means to "[love] thy neighbor as thyself" (Luke 10:27) as I was that night when, as a fifteen-year-old boy, I watched a prophet of God reach out to restore the self-confidence and self-esteem of a young man who had made a simple but embarrassingly obvious mistake. Had I not been in that meeting, I would have missed the single event that taught me more about loving God's prophets than any other experience. I will be forever grateful that I attended.

Similar experiences take place every Sunday in wards and branches throughout the Church. For example, consider the following incident, as described by a young man shortly before he left for his mission:

My single most influential Church leader, during my early years, was my Sunday School teacher when I was eleven. She was short and fat and wasn't very pretty. We made fun of her all the time, mainly because we were all bigger than she, and we were only eleven!

One Sunday, when we began to misbehave, she stopped talking. We immediately quieted down. She then told us about her childhood, about the problems she had faced while growing up, and about how she had decided at a very young age to do everything Heavenly Father asked of her. She then bore her testimony, and concluded by pleading with us to live the gospel and keep the commandments.

The impact of what she said was profound. I remember that experience vividly. I remember how she looked. I remember where she stood. I don't have any idea what she said, in terms of specifics, but I certainly remember how I felt. I remember thinking, "This is the neatest lady I have ever known," and I knew that I loved her.

That experience changed my entire attitude toward the Church. I didn't know what was happening at the time, but I knew how I felt. I also knew it was a better feeling than anything I had experienced before. I thought, "If that is what the prophet meant when he told us that Heavenly Father would bless us if we kept his commandments, then that is what I want to do," and later that day I knelt in prayer and promised him that I, too, would do as he asked. I have often thought how much I would have missed had I not attended church that Sunday.

President Kimball said, "There is no compulsion in one going to meetings or to praying or to having home evening, or to living the law of the Sabbath or any of the other laws of the Ten Commandments or the other scores of commandments, but the Lord seems to know what will make people supremely happy, and he has outlined a program which will develop and give growth to the people."[3] Worshiping the Lord in church meetings provides rich opportunities for young people to have spiritual experiences. Thus we need to do all in our power to make certain they take advantage of those opportunities.

14

Family Home Evening

"Son, we're ready to start." I had told Mom four times already that I had too much to do. I had three exams the next day, and my senior project in English was due on Thursday. To top it off, my obnoxious little brother was about to get his nose broken. Sometimes I felt like punching his lights out! The last thing I needed that night was to spend an hour in family home evening.

Mom had told me I didn't have to attend if I didn't want to. Some choice. Although I believed her about the choice business, I learned a long time ago that whenever I didn't do what I was supposed to do, I ended up feeling miserable. "I'll be there in a minute," I groaned.

Fortunately the opening song was "Love at Home," one of my favorites. Brian, whose turn it was to conduct, called on Mom for the opening prayer. As always, she talked with the Lord as if he was present. My mother has always had a special gift for doing that. As she prayed, I thought about how tough it is to be divorced with three teenagers. What a great lady. She's my best friend.

Sarah gave the lesson on the importance of obedience and talked about a family that was blessed because they obeyed the Lord. We also read some scriptures. She did a nice job, and I felt proud.

Mom then shared some of the sacred experiences she'd had when she was growing up. As she spoke, I thought about how much I loved her. As she concluded the lesson, she told us how

106

much she loved us, how important we were to her, and how she wanted us to be together forever. By the time she finished, it was hard for me to talk. I felt that special, warm feeling I feel mostly when I am with my family and at Church, and I knew that I'd rather be at home with those three people than anywhere else in the world.

Family Home Evening

In 1915 President Joseph F. Smith introduced the "weekly home evening program," and with it came the following promise to the members of the Church: "If the Saints obey this counsel, we promise that great blessings will result. Love at home and obedience to parents will increase. Faith will be developed in the hearts of the youth of Israel, and they will gain power to combat the evil influences and temptations which beset them."[1] Thus, the predecessor of the family home evening program was established. The prophets since that time have consistently re-affirmed President Smith's promises and counseled family members to meet together to increase spirituality and strengthen family bonds.

Family home evening is a Churchwide program designed to help families learn the gospel, love one another, and develop a sense of family unity. The Lord has promised great blessings to those who follow his counsel to hold regular family home evenings. In summarizing the potential of the program, Elder Dallin H. Oaks said, "It is a striking fact that the family home evening is the ideal time to accomplish almost every type of family togetherness. It is the ideal place for the family to pray together, learn together, counsel together, play together, and even work together. Most of us recognize this, but I wonder how many of us are really using the family home evening to its full potential."[2]

In order to help families enjoy the benefits that come from effective family home evenings, the Church has published the *Family Home Evening Resource Book*. In describing the potential of this publication, Elder Oaks said:

> More than any prior manual, the *Family Home Evening Resource Book* is designed to accomplish the broadest purposes of the family home evening. . . . [This book] is a

superior resource for parents to use in fulfilling their parental responsibilities and for family fun and learning. It is not a book just to own or to store on a shelf. It is a book to be used. Make sure you have it in your home. Use it. It will bless your lives and the lives of your children.[3]

Unfortunately, many parents do not take advantage of the rich gold mine contained in the *Family Home Evening Resource Book*. In fact, some don't even know it exists. As a father of three confessed:

We struggled with family home evening for three years and made no headway. After hearing about a friend's positive experience with the *Family Home Evening Resource Book*, we decided to buy one. Only then did I learn thad we'd had a copy on our shelf for two years. How embarrassing! After using it for a year, we were convinced that the material is so great that it's worth buying two and giving one away (which is what we did with our extra). I can't say enough good things about that publication. The material in that book has changed the way we have family home evening.

However, the *Family Home Evening Resource Book*, like all other tools designed to help us rear our children in light and truth, is *only* a resource. To meet the specific needs of our families, we must adapt these ideas to the ages and circumstances of our children. One father explained it this way:

The secret to our success has been flexibility, so our methods have constantly changed as our children have grown. I once heard President Kimball say that if eight things were present, we'd have a quality family home evening: a lesson, scripture reading, music, stories, an activity, prayers, refreshments, and a relaxed atmosphere with no criticism. Over the years we've found that this formula has always worked, as long as we allow enough flexibility to meet our children's needs.

For example, we've been particularly flexible in our activities. When holidays roll around, we have our own family parties. At other times we've played games, made posters for school, prepared talks for church, and watched video movies, particularly those put out by the Church. We've gone to the zoo, visited historic sites, and even had our own family track meets in the back yard. Recently we spent several weeks assembling our seventy-two-hour emergency-preparedness kits. We've also had service projects for those in need. Our goal has been to create as many positive, happy memories for our children as possible. However, we've never let the activities take priority over teaching our children the gospel. The activities are the dessert. But we've always served them some of the meat of the gospel, so they could have some spiritual experiences.

Music also plays an important role in successful family home evenings. As a young mother explained: "Singing is an essential part of every family home evening, simply because it is such an easy way to bring the Spirit into our home. We have opening and closing hymns. We also have a "Fun Songs" section, where each person chooses a favorite song and the rest of the family sings along. Some songs are unique; some are downright bizarre. But they create happy memories for everyone. That's what's important."

Regular family home evenings also give children clear messages about their value to their families and their worth as individuals. Often this message is more clearly spoken by example than by precept. Consider the message that regular family home evenings gave to one junior-college coed:

There was never any doubt in my mind that we were important to my parents. Even though they were both extremely busy, we had family home evening every Monday night. No exceptions. Interruptions were not allowed. No TV. No phone calls. No radio. No outside appointments. I heard my dad decline meetings with very important people when they wanted to meet on Monday night. That was our night together, and it was sacred. My folks also spent hours preparing for the lessons. They would never have put in that kind of time on somebody they didn't think was important.

Under such conditions, bonds of love are developed, and

109

the foundation for happiness and family solidarity is entrenched in the lives of family members. As a fourteen-year-old girl explained:

My friends think we have the neatest family in the world. They can't believe that we do so much together and love each other like we do. I mean, it's just beyond them to really believe that I love my little brother. Three of them have little brothers, and they hate them! They would also never think of talking about their boy friends around the dinner table; but I do it all the time. The reason I can do it is that I trust my family. They are really my best friends, the only ones that I can always count on.

Despite our best intentions, however, things don't always go right. This often happens when we stop listening to our children. Although running a business without listening to our customers would be unthinkable, we often try to run family home evening without input from our children. A mother described her difficulties with trying to run family home evening:

As our children got older, family home evening became painful, particularly for our two teenagers, so my husband and I sat down with them privately to find out what was going on. As they saw it, we did the same old thing every week, with almost everything geared to the younger children. They couldn't talk about things that interested them. They had no opportunity to participate. We preached a lot. The meetings lasted too long. And we fed them no "gospel meat." In short, we had missed the mark completely. Our approach had worked ten years ago, but we had gotten into a rut.

That night things changed. Based on their observations, we limited the lessons to fifteen minutes, and each meeting lasted no longer than one hour. A new assignment wheel identified who did what: opening song, opening prayer, lesson, activity, refreshments, closing song, closing prayer. The wheel rotated each week, so everyone got to contribute in different ways. My husband and I served as resources. If the children wanted help, they asked for it. Otherwise, they were on their own. Where possible, we let the older

110

children help the younger ones prepare, which involved them more and gave them a stake in our success. We added a question-and-answer period, where everyone could ask gospel questions and see if they could stump Dad—a goal they regularly achieved. That alone gave us a great, although subtle, excuse to study the gospel in ways we had not done before.

We also introduced a new game called "What do you like about this person?" We rotated through the family, focusing on a different person each week. We all thought of as many positive things as we could about the person and then bombarded him or her with the information.

All of a sudden, family home evening became exciting. The children loved the new format, and our regular feedback sessions provided information for midcourse corrections. We were amazed at how much our family home evenings came to life when we started listening to our children and responding to their needs.

When children present the lessons, they internalize the principles much more easily. They also feel a sense of pride and satisfaction with having accomplished something important. A young man reported just before he left for his mission: "When I was six, I gave a lesson on 'judge not that ye be not judged.' As a part of that lesson, I told a story about Thumper, the little rabbit in the movie *Bambi*. I can still remember what I said that night. I spent a lot of time preparing that lesson, and I was very proud of it. It has stuck with me forever. It was one of the first things I ever did that was *really* grown up."

By teaching our children the gospel in regular family home evenings, we ensure blessings for ourselves and for our posterity for generations to come.

During the week following the First Presidency's 1915 request that families meet together weekly to study the gospel, Ida went to the bedroom window of their small farmhouse and talked with Peter, her husband, who was cleaning the weeds from the ditch on the north side of their home. She said, "Father, President Joseph F. Smith has asked us to meet together each week to study the gospel with our children. What do you think?" Peter responded, "I think that we should follow the prophet." The next Sunday Peter and Ida began holding weekly "home hours" with their children, a practice that they continued every week until their last child left home to serve as a missionary in Switzerland thirty-eight years later.

Not coincidentally, seven of their ten children served missions. All ten were married in the temple. Nineteen of twenty-one grandsons served missions; and of their thirty-five grandchildren, only one has a marriage which has not been sealed in the temple. Seventy-five years later their posterity of several hundred now rise up and call them blessed for their faithfulness and devotion in following the prophet.

The Lord keeps his promises! Even under difficult circumstances, the Lord will pour out his blessings upon families who are obedient and who faithfully teach their children the gospel. President Kimball illustrated the blessings that come from family home evenings:

Many years ago we went to one of the Iron Curtain countries when we were touring the world. . . . We attended a series of meetings at which many people were in attendance. My first questions to these faithful Saints were these: "How do you get along with your children? Are they taught about God in their school?"

They said, "No. The teachers teach them that there is no God and teach them many other things that are opposed to what we believe."

Then I asked, "If every day the children receive that kind of training, how do you keep them faithful to the Church?"

One of the brethren said, "We're holding our children. They still go on missions, they still believe in God, they still pray, and they still do all of the things that are required of good Latter-day Saint boys and girls. We, as parents, provide good homes for them and continue to teach and train them righteously. Therefore, what they hear in the daytime from a godless school teacher makes no difference to them. It just runs off like water on a duck's back."

112

When children go off to school or to play with their friends, parents cannot be totally sure of what they are learning. But if parents take time at home each evening to explain the gospel program to their children, it will offset the negative things they may get during the day.[4]

15

The Value of Service

"I just can't do it," I complained to my dad. "No way!"

"Sure you can. Besides, you promised Bishop Larson you'd do it. Every fourteen-year-old boy ought to enjoy the excitement of speaking in sacrament meeting."

"Come on, Dad. I don't want that kind of experience. Besides, I wouldn't know what to say."

"You have a testimony, don't you?"

"Of course. But that doesn't mean that I would have anything to say in sacrament meeting."

"You believe in giving service, don't you?" he asked.

"Sometimes. It all depends on who it's for."

"Well, one way you can render service to the other members of this ward is to share your testimony with them. Don't worry. You'll do a great job."

"What if I get sick?"

"That won't be a problem. They'll just let you give your talk the next week."

I knew I was trapped. There was no way I could weasel out of this one.

Two weeks later I found myself sitting on the stand. They had just finished passing the sacrament, and Bishop Larson, who stood less than ten feet away, announced me as the next speaker. I was out of breath by the time I reached the pulpit. As I started to read my talk, the fear left me. The words came easily as I told the congregation about the importance of friendship and how much

114

I appreciated everyone in my teachers quorum. As I bore my testimony, I felt the Holy Ghost stronger than I had ever felt it before. Dad was right when he promised me that if I accepted this assignment, the Lord would bless me with a great spiritual experience.

The Blessings of Service

The scriptures clearly teach us that when we serve one another, we are really serving God. (See Mosiah 2:16–17). Unselfish service magnifies our souls and invites the Spirit of the Lord into our lives. Indeed, one of the major reasons for calling people to positions of responsibility in the Church is to provide them with opportunities to serve; and by doing so, they enjoy the gifts of the Spirit.

Parents have a sacred obligation to teach children the joy of service, and the home is where these lessons can best be learned. As King Mosiah said, "Ye will teach [your children] to walk in the ways of truth and soberness; ye will teach them to love one another, and to serve one another." (Mosiah 4:15.) The easiest way to teach this important lesson is by example. As they watch us enjoy serving others, they will better understand the Savior's statement, "Whosoever will be chief among you, let him be your servant." (Matt. 20:27.) As a young mother explained:

My mother often took me along when she went visiting teaching. When we lived in Illinois, she visited Sister Gonzalez. I will never forget listening to them trying to communicate. Mother spoke no Spanish. Sister Gonzalez spoke no English. Nobody understood anybody; but they loved each other, and the Spirit was there. My mother told me over and over again that when we served Sister Gonzalez, we were really serving Heavenly Father. As I watched my mother love and serve others, both inside and outside the family, I developed that same love myself.

By rendering unselfish service, we put ourselves in a position to receive a witness of the Spirit that what we have done is consistent with the mind and will of God. Many less active young people have been touched by those feelings and, as a result, have gained testimonies of the gospel. A senior in high school shared the following experience:

> I wasn't active in the Church as a child. However, when I was in the ninth grade, the teachers quorum had a service project of painting the outside of an older couple's home. They invited me to participate, so I spent the entire day with those guys. It was great. I also felt some feelings that I had never felt before, particularly when Brother and Sister Whitney told us how much they appreciated what we did for them. That day was the turning point for me, and I have been active ever since.

Another young man had a similar experience while unselfishly serving others:

> One of my favorite people is a divorced woman with four teenage children. In addition to working full-time and caring for her children, she unselfishly helped others in many quiet ways. In terms of her priorities, however, her yard came last. So we decided to do something about it.
>
> At 7:00 A.M. one Saturday morning, seven of us showed up at her home with rakes, shovels, hoes, and a power lawn mower. Five hours later her yard was spotless.
>
> I will never forget the look on her face when she came outside and saw us working. She couldn't believe that seven guys would care enough to spend their Saturday morning helping her. I will also never forget how I felt while we worked that morning. I had a similar feeling when I was baptized for the dead on our last temple trip.

Rendering righteous service to others lifts our souls and invites the Spirit of the Lord to come into our lives. In fact, that is the only way some blessings come. As President Spencer W. Kimball said, "Only when you lift a burden, God will lift your burden. Divine paradox this! The man who staggers and falls because his burden is too great can lighten that burden by taking on the weight of another's burden. You get by giving, but your part of giving must be given first."[1] A senior in high school described how she learned that valuable lesson:

> I will never forget the worst day of my life. I broke up

with my boyfriend, failed two tests, and didn't get a part in the school production. In addition, one of my best friends started some ugly rumors about me. I wanted to die.

When I got home from school, I remembered that my mom and I were scheduled to spend three hours that evening at the local nursing home with some elderly people. That was the last thing I wanted to do that night. But I had no choice. We'd told them the week before that we would do it.

I also remembered what my father had told me on many occasions: "When the world seems to have fallen in on you, find someone who needs help and go to work. The Lord will bless your efforts, and it will amaze you how much better you'll feel afterward." So I went.

I spent part of that evening reading to the sweetest little man I had ever met. The rest of the time was spent with a lady in a wheelchair who had no family within a hundred miles.

As I drove home that night, a sweet, peaceful feeling came over me. In my mind I heard the words of the Master: "Inasmuch as ye have done it unto one of the least of these my brethren, ye have done it unto me." (Matt. 25:40.) All of my problems weren't solved; but I felt confident that I could handle them and that things would turn out okay.

The Lord consistently blesses both the giver and the receiver when we manifest our willingness "to bear one another's burdens, that they may be light." (Mosiah 18:8.) A newly ordained priest described how unselfish service blessed a young woman and her mother:

Last year a friend of mine joined the Church. Although her nonmember mother wasn't hostile, she didn't hide the fact that she cared little for the Church.

Three months later the girl and her mother moved to another part of town. They blocked out all day Saturday and Sunday to get everything moved — and even then they doubted if that would be enough time. I called the president of our elders quorum for help.

At 7:30 A.M. on Saturday morning, ten guys showed up

117

with four trucks. Combined with the five people in our family, we almost had an army! The mother was so touched by our thoughtfulness that she spent most of the morning crying. She just couldn't believe that so many people whom she didn't even know would treat her so kindly. By 11:00 A.M. everything they owned had been moved into their new home.

That single incident caused a miraculous transformation in the mother. She began meeting with the missionaries, and four months later she was baptized.

One of the great benefits of unselfish service is spiritual experiences. When we serve others, we place ourselves in a position to receive revelation much more quickly than would otherwise be the case. The service need not be highly visible. In fact, the most meaningful service is often rendered quietly, as a result of the Spirit's gentle promptings. A grandfather learned this lesson as a young man and described his experience this way:

> Twenty-five years ago, after a general priesthood meeting, I felt impressed to stop by Susan's apartment. I was eighteen at the time and felt a little awkward dropping by unannounced. However, Dad had repeated over and over to me the importance of following the promptings of the Spirit, especially when they came as strong as that one did. So I did as I was "told."
>
> After we were seated, I told Susan about the great meeting I had just attended and asked if she would like me to share my notes with her. She agreed, so I proceeded to summarize each of the speeches.
>
> As I spoke, her eyes filled with tears. Later I learned that her boyfriend had invited her to be immoral with him later that evening, and she had agreed. As I spoke, the Spirit bore witness to her of the enormity of the mistake she was contemplating, and she resolved at that moment to never see her boyfriend again.
>
> Recently I got a letter from Susan. She wrote in part, "I have since married a wonderful man in the temple and have five delightful children. I have often thanked my Heavenly

Father for your visit that night. By following the promptings of the Spirit, you served as an instrument in the hands of the Lord to help me prevent what would have been the most tragic mistake of my life. I can never repay him for what he did for me."

I have no idea what I said that meant so much to her, nor is that important. I have learned, however, the truth of Elder Boyd K. Packer's statement, "Inspiration comes more quickly when we need it to help others than when we are concerned about ourselves."[2] With only few exceptions, every revelation I have ever received has come while serving others.

As we teach our children to serve, it is important that we teach them to serve for the right reasons. Serving the Lord because we expect a tangible reward or the approval of others is one thing. Serving because we love the Lord is another thing entirely. For such people, service is a measure of their pure love of Christ. A high councilor recalled this illustration:

> Years ago, when I was called to teach an early-morning seminary class, I had the responsibility to select a seminary president. After consultation with the bishop, we felt impressed to call James, the seventeen-year-old son of the ward clerk.
>
> This young man knew what service was all about because his parents had taught by both precept and example. For instance, during the five previous years, Jim and his father had been home teachers to four widows. The two of them were always there when somebody in the ward needed help. He also mowed the chapel lawn once each week.
>
> When I asked Jim about the service he had rendered, he said, "It isn't that big a deal. When we help other people, we are really serving the Lord. It's one of the ways we show our love for the Lord. I'm sure I could have done a lot more." I then asked him how he felt about the Savior, and he started to weep. After a few minutes, he whispered, "I love him." This kid was doing the right thing for the right reason.

When we have the pure love of Christ in our lives, we serve

with a purity of heart that sanctifies our service and blesses both the giver and the receiver. When we teach our children to serve others, we teach them to serve the Lord and keep his commandments. That puts them in a position to enjoy spiritual experiences that strengthen testimonies and bless lives.

16

The Covenant Interview

My watch said one A.M., and I was very nervous. As the traffic light turned green, I saw a pay phone in the middle of the next block. "Would you please stop at that telephone on the right and let me call home!"

Randy gripped the steering wheel tighter, looked at me, and growled, "Stephanie, what's this nonsense? You're a senior in high school, for heaven's sakes. I mean, it's not like you're a little kid anymore." I heard Pam and Jim giggle from the back seat.

"Will you please do as I asked? It will only take a few minutes."

"So we're going to be forty-five minutes late. What's the big deal?"

"The big deal is that we told my folks that we would be home by one o'clock. We aren't going to make it, and I don't want them to worry."

"We couldn't help it that the waiter took his time getting the food to us after the dance. It also isn't our fault that the man's car wouldn't start without help. What we did was honorable. I mean, your folks will think we're wonderful for helping him."

"Randy, you need to understand something. Three weeks ago my mom and I had a covenant interview, and we talked about problems we had with each other. She has this problem. If I'm not home when I say I'll be home, especially after a date, she worries. That's just the way she is. So I promised her I'd call if I was ever going to be late. If I don't, she won't trust me anymore. So please stop, and let me give her a call."

"All right," he said, smiling at me. "It's different than the way we do things at our house. But if it's important to you, let's get on with it."

What Is a Covenant Interview?

Several years ago Elder S. Dilworth Young visited our stake for a stake conference. In the course of his instructions to the stake and ward leaders, he described what he called a covenant interview with our children. This interview, held at least monthly (and more frequently if needed), normally lasts from thirty minutes to an hour. He called it a covenant interview because, as problems are discussed, each person makes promises or covenants concerning what he or she will do to address them. The covenants are then written down and become part of a permanent record that is available for future reference.

The term *covenant interview* is not intended to give the impression that this is an official term used by the Church. Although the word *covenant* usually refers to sacred pacts made between an individual and the Lord, the kinds of promises exchanged by parents and their children through an interview are clearly not in the same class.[1] However, they are agreements that parents and children make with each other and, therefore, can be called covenants. In addition, young people who participate in these interviews consistently report that they better understand the nature of covenants that they make with the Lord as a result of their experience in fulfilling their agreements and promises with their parents.

The major purpose of the covenant interview is to let children know that we love them and that they are of infinite worth before Heavenly Father. By holding these interviews, we and our children can communicate more effectively, solve problems that either may wish to address, learn gospel principles in ways that are relevant to our lives, give both of us an opportunity to hold one another accountable, strengthen the bond of love, give our children time to share spiritual experiences, and build esteem in our children.

The best way to begin a covenant interview is to kneel in prayer together, and then sit down, facing each other, and start talking. The easiest way to start is by saying, "What can I do to be a better parent?" and then listen to what our children tell us.

Covenant interviews can cover a variety of subjects. They almost always include, for example, a discussion of problems, such as difficulties in school, interpersonal problems with peers or family members, disagreement with family rules, frustrations with girlfriends or boyfriends, and basic information sharing. We and our children also decide on some promises to each other. An interview is a simple way for us to learn what's going on in our children's lives. If they have had some success experiences, this is a good time to talk about them. Essentially then, our discussion should address both our own and our children's needs; and anything that falls into that category is appropriate to talk about.

After discussing problems, successes, and achievements, we need to review the decisions we made in the last interview. The last item on the agenda, before kneeling in prayer, is to go over the commitments made during that interview, to ensure that both parties clearly understand the assignments and to guarantee that the written list is accurate. Remember, the major purpose of the covenant interview is to let our children know that we love them and that they are important to their Heavenly Father.

The Blessings Will Follow

Since Elder Young introduced the idea of holding covenant interviews, many parents in our stake have regularly conducted these interviews each month with their children; and several types of blessings have consistently resulted from these activities.

First, covenant interviews help us to hold our children accountable—one of the more important jobs a parent has—without looking like the "bad guy." The covenant interview format, with its written list that is reviewed during subsequent meetings, also ensures that *both* parent and child are held accountable.

Second, experience with covenant interviews is consistent with Elder Thomas S. Monson's belief that "When performance is measured, performance improves. When performance is measured and reported back, the rate of improvement accelerates."[2] As one father explained: "I can always tell when it's time for another covenant interview with my twelve-year-old daughter. All of the sudden the things that we talked about in our last interview start to get done. It's interesting to watch. The reason? She knows we will go over the things each of us promised to do; and she wants to be certain that she has kept her commitments."

A third blessing is that covenant interviews make administering discipline easier for parents. Since all agreements are reviewed regularly, responsible behavior gets noticed and can be immediately rewarded. On the other hand, the failures tend to be painfully obvious, and both the parent and the child tend to hold themselves accountable. This by itself substantially increases the potential for solving problems. Both can then work together to help each other do what each agreed to do. A single mother described the following interaction with her teenage son:

> For years I battled with my oldest son about the time he should get home from activities, and the problems got much worse as soon as he turned sixteen. He simply resisted deadlines and was continuously late. Finally I realized that I was doing all the worrying and fussing. It didn't bother him at all.
>
> In our monthly covenant interview, we discussed the problem. I told him that from now on I would no longer tell him what time to be home at night. We would negotiate it ahead of time. However, once we agreed on a time, that was the latest time that I expected him to arrive. If he wasn't there, and he didn't call to let me know why he would be late, he couldn't use the car for the next week.
>
> Since that time, we have had no problems with deadlines. He has been late only once; and his first comment, as he walked through the door was "I know. You don't have to say anything. But it's not going to happen again." What a relief. I'm no longer the bad guy. The problem is his, and he's willing to take the consequences.

A fourth blessing is that covenant interviews can deal with subjects too private for regular family home evenings and family councils. There are times when we can teach our children as a group, and there are times when a one-on-one relationship is best. For example, a father shared the following information about his sixteen-year-old son:

> Something had been bothering Jim for several weeks, but he wouldn't discuss it. The other family members asked him about it in our weekly family home evenings and in the family councils, but he refused to respond. I also told him privately that I would be happy to visit with him anytime he wanted to talk, but he took no initiative.
>
> After the first hour and a half of our covenant interview, he finally raised the subject. The problem dealt with a minor transgression he had committed, and he didn't know how to deal with it. Eighty minutes later we both understood the problem, and he had a plan for resolving it. Although we understand that the confidential things we talk about in those interviews are kept confidential, he again swore me to secrecy and said that there was no other setting in which he could feel comfortable in addressing such a problem.

A fifth blessing is that covenant interviews help improve family decision making. Most children want to participate in or at least influence decisions that affect them, but few want the responsibility that comes with that participation. Effective covenant interviews make avoiding those responsibilities almost impossible. A fourteen-year-old girl reported the following:

> I know that if I can get my dad to agree to something in a covenant interview, I have a commitment I can depend on. All I have to say is, "Dad, you promised," and I have no question about whether he will do it. He always has, and he always will. It also puts pressure on me, because I can no longer ignore the things he asks me to do. If I don't like what's going on, I can have my say, and my parents listen. And most of the time, if I approach it right, I even get my way. But I can't do it anymore by sitting back and griping. I have got to get involved.

A sixth blessing is that covenant interviews give us an opportunity to talk with each of our children regularly. A major complaint in most families is the lack of one-to-one contact between parents and children because of differences in schedules and demands on parents' time. Regular biweekly covenant interviews, for example, ensure that children have access to their parents for at least one hour of uninterrupted time once every two weeks. A mother of six children shared this insight with us:

> Schedules are so hectic at our home that we seldom have even dinner together, let alone the luxury of spending private time visiting with each other one to one. That is why covenant interviews are so important. My children and I treat them just like regular Church meetings and build them into our schedules. I can get more done with my children in an hour of covenant interview time than I can in a month with our regular schedule.

As a seventh blessing, regular covenant interviews build trust. The more we and our children trust each other, the fewer problems we will have with rebellion and disobedience. If our children see that we have consistently behaved in a trustworthy manner, they will probably trust us and be more inclined to do what we ask. It works the other way around too, as one single parent discovered:

> I am finally learning to trust my son. That is a big relief, because this is the first time I've felt that way in years. I realize now that we have been talking past each other for a long time. As a result, he did not trust me, and I did not trust him. It is unfortunate how those misunderstandings arise. If I had started these interviews with him when he was six, most of the difficulties we have faced could have been prevented. It is a wonderful feeling to finally have my son trust me once again.

An eighth blessing is that covenant interviews are the easiest way that we know for dealing with conflict and for solving problems. If both the parent and child agree to deal with problems when they are small, the child has given "permission" to talk about things that bother the parent (and vice versa). Note the following example of how one father deals with problems he has with his children:

The first question I ask each of my children is "What can I do to be a better dad?" They are brutally honest, and they always bring up things that I do that bug them. That information has been extremely helpful, because then I know what I need to do to resolve the problems. I honestly want to be a good father. Since they are consumers of my "fatherhood services," it makes sense to find out what they like and don't like. Of course some things aren't negotiable; but most things are. If changing a behavior or two will help me be more influential with my children, I certainly want to know what those things are. I would be foolish to ignore such valuable information. I have learned more about being a good father from that feedback than from any other source, except what I learned from my own father.

Dealing with problems goes both ways; I also have my day in court when I tell them about the things they're doing that I would like to see changed. It's amazing how much we can get done in those meetings. We can accomplish more in that setting than in any other format.

A ninth blessing is that covenant interviews provide both us and our children with regular reminders concerning strengths and the areas that may need improvement. The parent and the child can then use this information to make midcourse corrections, as it were, to improve behavior and to make certain that both are on the right track. This is particularly helpful in developing better habits. As one mother reported,

> Reviewing the commitments we made during the last session automatically builds in opportunities to provide my son with positive feedback. That is one of the most beneficial parts of those interviews—I have a chance to concentrate on the positive and to reinforce the things that he does well without appearing to be gushy or patronizing. The evidence is there, and his success is equally apparent to both of us. That helps build self-esteem. He now knows he can succeed at just about anything he tries because he has a track record of success. If I have to deal with something negative, there are plenty of positive things in the overall interview so the time doesn't appear to be a scolding session. For every

mistake he makes, he probably does a hundred things well. I refuse to give the negative things equal time.

A tenth blessing is that covenant interviews help everyone involved to communicate more easily. As children get older, the interviews commonly become both less formal and much more frequent. A divorced father reported the following about his relationship with his son:

> We hold formal covenant interviews once every month for no more than an hour. However, we hold informal interviews several times a week, and they often last two or three hours. My son knows he can count on me to listen, to suggest alternatives, to provide help if asked and to stay out of his business unless I am invited in. He also knows that he can trust me under all circumstances. It's great to have a "best-friend" relationship with my children.

An eleventh blessing is that covenant interviews teach children the importance of keeping covenants. We live in a world where people cheat, lie, steal, and don't trust each other. Promises don't mean much anymore. The Lord wants a people who are pure and who can be trusted to keep their covenants. Since covenant interviews include promises that children and parents make with each other, the meetings provide an ideal forum for helping children understand the importance of keeping their word and doing what they say they will do. A returned missionary explained it in the following way:

> You know, I have come to appreciate the word *covenant*. All through my teenage years, I had covenant interviews with my dad and mom. Each month I promised them I would do certain things, and they also made promises to me. They always kept their promises. I kept most of mine; and it got better as I got older.
>
> As a result, the word *covenant* took on a very personal and important meaning. I learned early in life that if I promised somebody something, I had a sacred obligation to keep that promise. The quality of my relationship with them depended on it.
>
> Then, when I went through the temple before my mis-

sion, I saw first-hand what my folks had been trying to teach me all those years. My relationship with my Father in Heaven depended upon how well I kept the covenants I had made with him. I have learned that making covenants is one of the most important things that can happen in life.

Doing It Right

There are several things we can do to make covenant interviews work well. First, we need to make sure that our children know that we love and trust them. We must sincerely want to help our children solve problems, and the importance of a supportive attitude cannot be overstated. Without it, the covenant interview could easily result in our children feeling as if we're their enemy. Unfortunately, covenant interviews can provide an opportunity for parents who are disposed to taking advantage of their children's increased vulnerability to punish them for their mistakes. Force and unrighteous dominion should be avoided at all costs.

On the other hand, supportive covenant interviews will help build a relationship that can be achieved in few other ways. As one father explained, "I have been able to get closer to my children as a result of regular covenant interviews than by any other means."

Second, covenant interviews must be held regularly, and the time spent must be free of interruptions. This is critical, since the child receives a clear message about his or her importance when we choose to respond to unknown telephone callers during the special times that are supposed to be set aside exclusively for parent and child.

Third, we must take time to prepare intellectually and spiritually for the meeting, particularly if there is an age span among our children. Prayer should also be part of that preparation.

Fourth, we can make keeping written records easier by having a notebook handy or by using a computer. Writing down commitments helps both the parent and child crystallize their thinking and clarify exactly what is really meant. The written product is also something tangible to which both the parent and child can refer and by which they can measure success. It tells exactly what is expected and when. As one mother explained, "I find that if things get down on paper, they will almost always get done. Writing things down forces us to specifically identify behaviors that need to be changed. That always makes change much easier. After a while, those positive changes become habits, and we eventually drop them from the list of commitments."

Fifth, we must be willing to hold our children accountable and to ask the difficult "why" questions when assignments are not completed. Even more important, we must be willing to be held accountable ourselves. We too will have assignments; by following through on them, we not only set an example of dependability and responsibility, but also demonstrate to the child that he or she can trust us to keep our promises.

Sixth, we must keep the format flexible, both in frequency and in content, so that the interview will meet the needs of all our children. We must understand each child's needs and deal with each one at his or her level. As President Lorenzo Snow explained, "A father, in communicating counsel to his son, should in the first place prepare himself to communicate those proper counsels which will suit the condition of his son."[3]

An interview with a three-year-old may require nothing more than a few moments of holding and kissing the child, a short visit about Heavenly Father's love for his children, and the parent and child kneeling in prayer together. A sixteen-year-old, on the other hand, may need a three-hour meeting to work through problems, to better understand a gospel principle, or to help him or her gain the skills and confidence to cope with unhealthy peer pressures and resist standards inconsistent with gospel principles. Understandably, then, we should give our children some say in how covenant interviews can best be used in our families. That flexibility is illustrated by the two following sample agreements. The first is a covenant between a father and his seven-year-old son:

Date: January 3

Invocation: Daniel

1. Dad won't put his arm in front of the TV while Daniel plays video games.

2. Daniel will hang up his clothes when he takes them off at night.

3. Dad will lie on the bed and visit with Daniel every night before Daniel goes to bed.

4. Daniel will use a tissue whenever he picks his nose.

5. Daniel will hurry faster when getting ready to go places so people won't have to wait for him.

Benediction: Dad

Compare the above items to those discussed with the same father and his seventeen-year-old son:

Date: February 13

Invocation: Andrew

1. Dad will try not to talk harshly to Andrew. If Dad should slip, Andrew will say, "Dad, you're talking harshly to me again."

2. Andrew will listen to Dad, so Dad won't have to talk harshly in order to get his attention.

3. Dad and Andrew will continue to do things alone, just the two of them.

4. Andrew will get going on his Scouting. Specifically, he will complete two merit badges by the next covenant interview.

5. Andrew will get his seminary assignments completed by March 1.

Benediction: Dad

These commitments can be extended indefinitely, depending on the needs of the parent and the child. One mother told us that the covenant interview agendas with her daughter regularly included over thirty items; and eighty percent of those items are on the agenda because of her daughter's insistence. Most agendas will be much shorter, but remember to be flexible when the situation calls for adjustments.

Seventh, we must be willing to listen to our children, both intellectually and emotionally. Some problems require nothing more than a listening ear. Others necessitate immediate action.

Eighth, we must be willing to empathize with and to express

love to our children. The power of love cannot be overemphasized. People will do positive things because of love that they will not do for any other reason. President Joseph F. Smith explained:

> Fathers, if you wish your children to be taught in the principles of the gospel, . . . if you wish them to be obedient to and united with you, love them! and prove to them that you do love them by your every word or act to them. For your own sake, for the love that should exist between you and your boys — however wayward they might be, . . . when you speak or talk to them, do it not in anger; do it not harshly, in a condemning spirit. Speak to them kindly; get down and weep with them, if necessary, and get them to shed tears with you if possible. Soften their hearts; get them to feel tenderly towards you. Use no lash and no violence, but . . . approach them with reason, with persuasion and love unfeigned. With these means, if you cannot gain your boys and your girls, . . . there will be no means left in the world by which you can win them to yourselves.[4]

Ninth, covenant interviews provide a splendid opportunity for parents and their children to share spiritual experiences. As they kneel together in prayer, express their love for one another, talk about the weightier matters of the kingdom, and communicate heart to heart, the Spirit of the Lord can be poured out powerfully and bear witness of the truth of the gospel and the love that a kind Heavenly Father has for them.

Finally, covenant interviews provide an invaluable opportunity to help build our children's self-esteem. A major function of the gospel is to help members understand their relationship with their Father in Heaven. Once a child understands his or her relationship to Heavenly Father, the desire to keep his commandments significantly increases.

Concentrating on our children's strengths, emphasizing the positive, and creating opportunities for successful experiences also motivate our children to excel. Keep in mind that a positive, permanent change in behavior is always accompanied by an increase in self-esteem.

ing goes on constantly in all families, through both
examples and counsel. But children need to learn both the doctrine and the application of the gospel in their lives. We need to
ascertain what our children need to learn, and then choose our
strategies accordingly.

What If the Covenant Interview
Doesn't Go according to Plans?

Not all plans work perfectly, and many run into what appear
to be difficult obstacles. The covenant interview can be an effective
method of developing responsibility and closer family ties. But
what happens if the problem the interview is to resolve is chronic
and the agreement is breached? Here's how one father handled
that difficulty:

> I stopped reading, looked at the clock, and realized that
> my fifteen-year-old son and I had a serious problem. He
> was thirty minutes late getting home. I put down the news-
> paper, went to the other room, and picked up the phone.
> When I finally heard my son's voice, I said, "John, are you
> lost?"
> "What do you mean?"
> I said, "I think you know what I mean. I'll see you in a
> minute."
> Five minutes later, John walked through the front door. I
> said, "Sit down. You and I are going to have a covenant inter-
> view."
> "A what?"
> "A covenant interview. That means we're going to talk
> about some problems, and we're going to write down what
> we decide." John had refused to acknowledge the fact that
> we have a right to know, before he leaves our home, where
> he is going, who he will be with, and when he will be back.
> Instead, he sneaks off. So we spent the next forty-five min-
> utes in a critical interview about responsibility.
> After we had prayer, the first thing I asked was, "John,
> what could I do to be a better father."
> Instantly he said, "Ease up."
> I was surprised at his response, since we really have very

133

few rules in our home. "Okay," I said, "I'll ease up. Tell me where."

He said, "You're too stiff. You won't let me go on any dates."

I couldn't believe what I was hearing. This kid had never expressed an interest in girls in his life. He couldn't even get up the nerve to talk with a girl because he was afraid she'd think he was dumb. He also consistently maintained that he hated *all* females except his mother. So it's not like this dating business was really a pressing issue. "Hold it," I said. "I can't ease up on that. It's not my rule."

"What are you talking about? It is too."

"No, it isn't either. It's the prophet's rule. I can't ease up on those rules. I made that promise to Heavenly Father. When the prophet speaks, I'm going to do what he says. He's the one who counseled against dating before age sixteen."

"Are you sure he said that?"

"Yes. If you want to press the issue, I'll be happy to find the quotes. Otherwise, you can trust me. But he did say it."

"All right, I'll trust you."

I then said, "Okay. Now what else can I do to be a better father?"

"Ease up on your rules. Give me freedom."

"Okay, but freedom doesn't come for nothing. It has to be earned."

"What do you mean?"

"The more I trust you, the more freedom you have. Are you trustworthy now?"

He thought for a while. "About half," he finally responded.

"Then that means you're about half untrustworthy."

He hesitated, then said, "You're right."

It was a decisive interview. After additional discussion, he wrote down four things he promised he would do, and I wrote down what I would do. We both then signed the paper and dated it, and I said, "Okay, we have a follow-up interview two weeks from tonight."

134

He said, "I'll be there."

I said, "So will I."

Now I have held lots of interviews with my children, but I have never conducted a covenant interview. My children and I have had some great talks, but we've never written down what we decided. As a result, a lot of things don't get done. That covenant interview was a first important step, but I knew that John needed follow-up. He was really out of control in some areas at that time. The covenants he wrote down were the following:

John's promises:

1. No caffeine. (John can't sleep at night, so he wandered around this house at two in the morning. We finally pinpointed the problem. He loves Dr. Pepper, and he drinks it like he was at a watering trough. Therefore, he made the commitment to stay away from drinks containing caffeine.)

2. Lights out by 11:30, excluding the exceptions we discussed, i.e., if the family stays up late watching a video or a movie on TV.

3. No leaving home unless I let you know where I'm going, who I will be with, and when I will be home.

4. I will tell my folks the truth.

Dad's promise:

1. Be a little bit more loose, as John becomes more trustworthy. Ease up and don't lose my temper so easily.

John sat down at the table and wrote out his commitments in longhand. They were his promises—he had ownership for them. I wrote mine, then we signed them. What we had written down became a covenant between the two of us.

Well, I was both delighted and relieved. It looked as if the problem had finally been solved. However, I couldn't have been more wrong. The very next week that rascal broke two of his covenants.

I got home about 8:30 P.M. Just as I was pulling into the driveway, he was getting into our other car. "Where are you going?" I asked.

"I'm going over to Bill's house to jump on his trampoline."

"OK. Have a good time, but please be home by 11:30."
He said, "OK," and drove away.

Well, it turned out that rather than going to Bill's house
to jump on the trampoline, he went to Mark's house to
listen to music; and he told me a lie to get there. Furthermore, he didn't get home until after midnight.

Susan, my wife, waited up for him, and I went to bed.
In fact, she insisted that I go to bed. I think she was afraid
I'd get mad. She was right. At that point I was so angry
that I felt like throttling him.

The next morning Susan and I discussed the matter privately. She didn't think that the problem was all that serious; and when I suggested that we take away his driver's
license, which he had gotten two days earlier, she was
convinced that it was overkill on my part. It was simply
too harsh a penalty for what he had done. But she agreed
to support me.

A few minutes later, when the two of us met with John,
I started the discussion. "OK, what are we going to do
about this?"

He started to hem and haw a little bit. He then said,
"What's the big deal?"

I said, "The big deal is that you gave me your word of
honor that you would do something, and you didn't do it.
You made some covenants with me, which you didn't keep.
In fact, you even wrote them down on a sheet of paper,
and you signed it."

Susan said, "He did that?"

"Absolutely." I got up, went into my office, and got the
paper on which John had written his covenants and signed
his name. Susan suddenly became an instant convert. She
waved that sheet in front of his nose and said, "John, it's
right here. You promised!"

He protested, "Mom!"

"Don't 'Mom' me. You wrote it out yourself, and you
signed it."

"But Mom, you don't understand."

"I understand it perfectly. You promised that you would
do something. You gave your word. You wrote it down

136

yourself, and then you didn't do it. What do you think it means?"

Susan clearly saw what he was up to, and she didn't like it anymore than I did. It was at that moment that John realized he didn't have a chance.

There's a great advantage in having had him write it. As they say in the legal profession, the records speak for themselves. It took away the possibility that the meeting would become coercive. Nobody was dictating anything.

I said, "John, she's right. You're the one who agreed to it. Nobody told you to. You signed it."

Normally we would have had a major battle on our hands. But he didn't say a word. He knew he had made a mistake, and he was stopped dead in his tracks, so to speak. Just having that single sheet of paper changed the entire focus of the discipline. The meeting was transformed from a potentially destructive and damaging encounter, as far as my relationship with him was concerned, to a less negative, more instructive experience.

I said, "Because you broke two promises, John, the only choice we have is to say you can't drive anymore. Not for a long time. Probably not more than a year."

John turned pale, and in a voice only slightly louder than a whisper he asked, "Are you serious?"

I smiled. "No, but you can't drive for the next two weeks. I hope you can catch on to what you're really doing to yourself. You aren't doing anything to us by your lying. True, it's painful to us to see your dishonesty; but we're not hurt, at least not in the eternal sense. You're the guy that's really getting beat up by this process. I'd also like you to write a five-page report on lying, based on what's recorded in the scriptures. What does the Lord say about it? Why does he hate liars? How come Satan likes to get people to lie? That's one of his main tasks, you know. Satan really likes liars."

It was a long interview; and when we finished, John's driver's license was in my pocket. Quite frankly, the whole thing was very hard on us, and I disliked the results almost as much as he did. It meant that Susan and I had to take him everywhere. The place where he works is fifteen miles away. But the end result was worth it. He learned some valuable lessons in that process.

The report on lying opened his eyes to what he was doing. For example, it shook him up to read about Korihor. After he had completed the project, he said, "I didn't know so many things had been said about lying. I also didn't think you cared if I lied to you. I just figured you didn't want to know, so you wouldn't be bothered."

John has learned that giving his word is serious business and the consequences of not keeping his word are very real. We believe that teaching him that lesson when he's sixteen is a whole lot better than trying to deal with it when he's twenty or forty. Where else could he learn a lesson so powerfully and yet so inexpensively? If he lies to his boss, he'll get fired. If he lies to the mission president, he'll be a lousy missionary. If he cheats in school, he'll flunk the class and likely be expelled.

Having the written document is the easiest way I have ever seen to deal with serious problems. John was the one who made the rules; he was the one who set the goals and made the commitments, not me. So when he failed to do what he said he would do, Susan and I weren't the bad guys. The responsibility fell squarely on his shoulders.

That happened three months ago, and we haven't had a problem with him lying since that time. He's also kept every promise he's made to me in our covenant interviews. He has been a different kid.

17

The Value of Keeping Records

The phone rang at 7:20 on Sunday morning. I picked it up and heard the pleasant voice of the first counselor in our bishopric.
"Hi Carol. This is Bill Simpson. Is Alex there?"
"Yes, but he's still in bed. Would you like me to wake him?"
"How soon will he be getting up?" he asked.
"He said he'd set his alarm for 7:45, but sometimes that doesn't mean a whole lot."
"I know what you mean. Why don't you ask him to give me a call as soon as he gets up. As you're probably aware, he's scheduled to speak in sacrament meeting this morning. The other youth speaker is sick, so if he'd like to take a few minutes longer than usual, he's welcome to do so."
"This morning!" I gasped. "I didn't know anything about it. But I haven't seen him for more than ten minutes at a time since last Wednesday night."
"Would you please ask him to give me a call when he gets up?"
I agreed, said good-bye, and hung up the phone. I knew Alex wasn't prepared. He told us last Sunday that he was scheduled to speak in sacrament meeting, but I had the impression that his assignment was still two weeks away!
At 7:24 I was standing next to my son's bed. "I just got an interesting call from Brother Simpson."
With his eyes still closed, he groaned, "What did he want?"
"He tells me you'll be speaking in sacrament meeting this morning."

Alex's eyes popped open, and I knew I had his attention. Ninety seconds later he was on the phone with Brother Simpson. "Sure, I'd be happy to. Thanks for the opportunity." He then hung up the phone, walked over to the kitchen cupboard, opened up the cabinet door, and dropped two slices of bread into the toaster.

"Well, what are you going to do?"

He looked at me, smiled, and said, "I'm going to be the two youth speakers in sacrament meeting this morning. I have ten minutes."

"Can I be of any help?"

"Nope. But thanks anyway." I felt sick to my stomach. I couldn't give a decent ten-minute talk if I had a week to prepare, and my sixteen-year-old son thinks he can give one two hours from now?

Alex took the longest shower of his life, dressed, and left at 8:15 for his priests quorum presidency meeting. As he walked out the door, I asked, "Are you ready for sacrament meeting?" He again grinned and said, "I hope so."

I again felt that empty feeling in the pit of my stomach. Several years ago he had suffered from low self-esteem, and I wasn't sure how he would react if he fell on his face, so to speak. I didn't see how he could help but embarrass himself—just as I do whenever I stand at the pulpit. And I had years of experience.

The opening activities of sacrament meeting that day were the shortest in the history of the Church: no announcements, no business, short hymns. Then my son stood at the pulpit and started to speak:

> *In First Nephi, chapter three, verse seven, the prophet Nephi said, "I will go and do the things which the Lord hath commanded, for I know that the Lord giveth no commandments unto the children of men, save he shall prepare a way for them that they may accomplish the thing which he commandeth them." From my own experience, I can bear witness that the Lord does prepare the way for us to accomplish what he asks us to do.*

Alex then shared a personal experience from two years earlier, when the Lord had helped him do something he thought was

140

impossible and had blessed him for his obedience. It was a touching experience. The Spirit of the Lord was present as he spoke. He closed by bearing his testimony that the gospel was true.

I couldn't believe what I had heard. It was truly a wonderful talk.

As he joined the family after the closing prayer, I said, "Son, that was great. How did you do it?"

"Simple. I just read part of my journal."

The Importance of Keeping Records

Keeping records is essential to building spirituality in our homes. Records of our spiritual experiences provide a way to keep track of the Lord's blessings and allow our posterity to know those blessings. In short, records provide a rich pool of spiritual experiences on which family members will draw for generations to come.[1] Often we, like the priesthood leader who shared the following experience, overlook the impact of important events in our lives:

> For years our Church leaders had counseled us to keep journals and other family records. However, I assumed that such counsel applied only to Church leaders and people whose lives were far more active than mine. Besides, I had never experienced anything I thought worth recording. Then I happened upon the following statement by President Wilford Woodruff regarding the importance of recording personal experiences.
>
> "[When] Elders go forth upon missions to the nations of the earth, they have to enter into a regular warfare. The Lord pours out his Holy Spirit upon them and they war with the world, the flesh, and the Devil, with kings, princes, Lords, Presidents and rulers. He is cast into prison and the Lord delivers him. The Devil enters into some of his converts and he lays hands upon them and he casts them out. The saints are sick and he heals them. He prophesies in the name of the Lord and his words come to pass. Rulers declare that he shall not preach to the people on pain of death. He preaches the word of God and many believe, obey and rejoice in the Lord and he is protected by the

power of God. He goes upon the sea and storms rage and he calms the water and wind in the name of the Lord. He is shielded and guarded by angels of God all the day long and he knows the power of God is with him and reveals unto him all the evils that lie in his path. *And yet he does not view these great and important things of value enough to make a record of them to spend a short time in writing them and the circumstances and history of those blessings unto him are lost both to the present and all future generations.* Are these things right? I do not believe they are. I do not believe a man is justified in neglecting to record these things."[2]

This statement sunk deeply into my heart. I had never cast out devils, healed the sick, prophesied in the name of the Lord, or calmed the seas. However, I realized that the Lord had given me my own set of spiritual experiences, some of which I could not remember, simply because I had not bothered to write them down.

Records can be kept in a variety of different forms, including journals, scrapbooks, quotes by family members, personal histories, and minutes of family meetings, such as family home evening.

Journals

Journals should include a record of spiritual experiences, answers to prayers, ordinances performed, blessings given, and other faith-promoting events. What is recorded should be accurate and complete, particularly as it relates to ordinances of the priesthood. One man learned the value of recording spiritual experiences the hard way:

> While serving as a bishop several years ago, I received a call from a bishop in another state. A young man, whom I had watched grow up and whom I had ordained an elder several months earlier, was preparing to leave for his mission. He had been interviewed, and the missionary papers had been prepared. However, there was no record of his receiving the Melchizedek Priesthood. I had ordained him an elder while he was home for Christmas vacation, but the paperwork for the ordination originated in his own

142

ward. Unfortunately, nobody bothered to notify his bishop of the ordination.

With a great deal of confidence, I went to my journal because I knew I had recorded the event. However, my entry read, "Last month I conferred the Melchizedek Priesthood on Mark Walker and ordained him to the office of an elder." I was embarrassed and chagrined. Had I bothered to record the ordinance properly and in a timely manner, a great deal of trouble could have been avoided. All of a sudden I better understood how Nephi felt when the Savior asked, "How be it that ye have not written this thing?" (3 Ne. 23:11.)

Recording spiritual experiences in journals can also strengthen the faith of descendants for generations to come. Consider for a moment the impact of the following experience.

Shortly after I returned from my mission, I came across the following journal entry of my father, who had served in the Palestine-Syrian Mission:

"After World War II broke out, and the brethren called all of the missionaries home throughout the world. At the time there were only four missionaries in the entire mission. So the four of us, along with President and Sister Jacobs and their family, boarded a ship and headed for home.

"Shortly after we arrived at Marseilles, France, our ship was quarantined, and nobody would tell us why. So the other ships in the convoy left, and we were stuck in the Marseilles harbor.

"The next morning the quarantine was lifted, and we were allowed to proceed on our trip. As we sailed along, we saw the debris from a ship that had been blown up. Later we learned that the ship that took our place in the convoy was torpedoed by a German submarine. Had we not been quarantined, our ship would have been hit, and we would have all been killed. The Lord takes care of his missionaries."

Few experiences have had such a profound impact on me and my family as that incident, because it helped us understand how much Heavenly Father loved his missionaries in general, and my father in particular. I will be forever grateful that he took the time to record that experience.

President Spencer W. Kimball counseled, "Get a notebook, my young folks, a journal that will last through all time, and maybe the angels may quote from it for eternity."[3] I have no way of knowing if angels are quoting from my father's journal. But that story has been quoted by family members many times in family home evening, in auxiliary lessons, and in sacrament meeting talks. To us it is scripture, and the reality of that experience is as meaningful to us as any scripture we have ever read.

If keeping your own journal is no small task, then getting your children to keep journals can be an even greater challenge. For some parents, parting the Red Sea would be easier. But it is not an impossible task. The experience of a father of seven children illustrates this point:

> Every Sunday we have our children write in their journals. My wife interviews those who are too little and records their words. As soon as they learn how to write, we have them draw a picture and then use whatever words they know to describe what they just drew.
>
> How do we get them to do it? We bribe. We use the old "M&M" technique. Every Sunday afternoon we have a special treat—something my wife has made especially for the Sabbath. Sometimes she bakes donuts. Sometimes it's cookies. Sometimes it's a special dessert. Our policy is, "As soon as you finish writing in your journal, you can have the family treat." They don't have to write in their journals if they don't want to. They just don't get the family treat until they do.
>
> We started this Sunday activity eight years ago. At that time Jim, our oldest child, was ten. Last week he got his first journals out and spent three hours reading them. He couldn't believe what he had written. He couldn't believe that a kid so young could write something that profound.
>
> Our children have quoted from their journals in their talks in church. They have used them for lesson material in Primary and family home evening. They have referred

144

to them when writing papers for their classes in school. Their journals have become a record of their lives. By reading them, they are continuously reminded of the blessings the Lord has given to them. We also make sure that they use acid-free paper, available at the Church Distribution Center, and write with permanent ink.

Scrapbooks

Technically speaking, scrapbooks are blank books in which miscellaneous items, such as awards, newspaper clippings, pictures, and certificates, are collected and preserved. They differ from journals in that scrapbooks contain little written explanation. The items in scrapbooks speak for themselves. Ideally scrapbooks are neatly categorized by year and filed neatly in file drawers.

For most of us, however, our filing system is made up of boxes of memorabilia stored in the basement. Regardless of their location, the challenge is to arrange them in a way that is both accessible and useful. One mother discovered an easy way to organize her family's keepsakes:

> For years I had tried to get our junk organized; but the more I tried, the more discouraged I got. My need to do it perfectly prevented me from ever doing more than start. Thus the collection from our ten years of marriage stayed in eight big boxes in our storeroom.
>
> One day a friend showed me how she had resolved her problem. On one of her bookshelves was a row of three-ring binders containing clear plastic sheets with pockets of various sizes. Some sheets contained photographs. Others contained certificates, awards, and newspaper articles. Everything was easily accessible and well organized. I realized I had just discovered the answer to my problem.
>
> The following Saturday my husband and I attacked our "ten years' worth of junk." Eight hours later we had not only organized the contents of all eight boxes, but we had also categorized and labeled 2800 pictures. We then did the same with the materials each of us had brought to our marriage. All of that "junk" was now neatly filed by year in fifteen three-ring notebooks in one bookcase.

145

Our three children also have their own books, and everything that happens to them gets filed. They put in all their pictures and some of their school work. They have all of their medical information, the hospital and doctor bills at the time they were born, the I.D. wrist bands they got at the hospital, the letters that my wife and I each wrote to them on the days they were born.

Since that time our children have spent hundreds of hours looking through those notebooks. When they get jam on the pages, the plastic sheets can easily be wiped off without damaging the contents. As new pictures and mementos come along, they are easily added. It has been wonderful, and keeping records has become fun instead of drudgery.

Quotes from Children

Occasionally children make comments that are quotable. Some are humorous. Others are profound. Still others provide insight into who they are and the greatness of their potential. Great lessons can be learned from our children, if we will take time to listen. As the Savior said, "Those things which never have been revealed from the foundation of the world, but have been kept hid from the wise and prudent, shall be revealed unto babes and sucklings in this, the dispensation of the fullness of times."(D&C 128:18.) When those revelations come, we should take the time to write them down. A father of nine described how he and his wife handle this matter in his family:

My wife has a book in which she records every statement our children make that we think is clever or profound. For example, one day as I came home from work, my daughter came running to me. I picked her up and said, "Linda, you get more beautiful every time I see you. I don't know what I'm going to do with you." She put the palms of her hands on my cheeks and said, "Well, Daddy, I guess you'll just have to marry me in the temple."

We have hundreds of such statements. I have memorized many of them and use them regularly in talks and lessons. The greatest benefits, however, come to the children. They see themselves in an entirely different light when they understand some of the profound things they have said.

For example, tonight I read several of these quotes as our family sat around the dinner table. They giggled at all of the comments; and at a couple of them our daughter laughed to the point that she almost fell off her chair. She then said, "I don't remember saying any of those things. I was really a neat little kid, wasn't I!" That is one of the real payoffs. Each time our children read them, they are again impressed with how clever they are—and how important they are to us and to our Heavenly Father.

Personal Histories

Writing our own histories and including in them the details of our lives are important. However, getting a record of our parents, some of whom are in the twilight years of their lives, is also very important. Unfortunately, many older people have neither the skill nor the energy to write their histories. So if it is to be done at all, the children must take the initiative. There are both hard and easy ways to accomplish that task. One of the easiest ways, as a father of four testifies, is to record the person's life history on audiotape:

Shortly after President Kimball asked the members of the Church to write their personal histories, I began mine. However, I was having some major difficulties getting going. One day, while reading the Book of Mormon, I came across the following statement by the prophet Nephi: "Behold, I make an abridgment of the record of my father, upon plates which I have made with mine own hands; wherefore, after I have abridged the record of my father then will I make an account of mine own life." (1 Ne. 1:17.)

The impact of that statement was profound. I realized that I was working on the wrong project. I was supposed to be working on my father's history, not mine. I immediately called my father on the phone, told him that I would like to record his personal history, and suggested that we do it the following weekend. He resisted, maintaining that he didn't have enough information to talk for fifteen minutes. We started at nine on Saturday morning. By the end

147

of the day, we had eight hours of his life story on audiotape, and we hadn't even gotten him through the first grade. One year later, when the history was completed, we had twenty-five hours of recorded tape. The edited version resulted in 160 pages of single-spaced manuscript, which we have published and distributed to family members.

I have since completed eight such interviews with my older relatives. In each case they vehemently resisted but later found it an enjoyable and richly rewarding experience. All they had to do was visit with me and tell me about the important happenings in their lives. Some of those happenings are the commonplace dates, places, and experiences. However, without exception they all have shared profound ideas, important thoughts, and rich experiences that bless everyone who reads them, particularly their own posterity.

Videotapes of loved ones also provide needed information, along with the added dimension of recording who they are and how they look. In addition to factual information, they provide hours of entertainment to friends and family members. Eventually, these records become priceless, as one woman learned in a most dramatic way: "Four years ago my father and mother came to our home for Thanksgiving. During that visit we recorded both of their life stories on videotape. On the following Monday they returned to Idaho Falls, and one week later my father died suddenly of a heart attack. Words cannot express how grateful I am that we listened to the Spirit of the Lord and recorded his history."

Family Home Evening Records

In chapter fourteen we discussed the importance of family home evening. It seems only natural that families who properly hold those meetings would frequently have spiritual experiences. Although one cannot predict when spiritual experiences will take place, it is important to have them accurately recorded when they do happen.

Other experiences during family home evening could be categorized as golden moments that family members will cherish for years to come. Consider, for example, the following comments:

Every evening at approximately nine o'clock we gather in our living room and read the scriptures. Tonight we had a delightful but unusual experience. Rather than reading the Book of Mormon, as is our custom, we read from another book of scripture: the minutes of our family home evenings.

I believe that one of the most sacred meetings in the Church is family home evening. Therefore, since September 27, 1976, we have kept a careful record of what took place in those meetings. I am the self-appointed record keeper, and I record in a spiral notebook what happens each Monday night. We now have several volumes.

Little did I realize at the time I began how valuable these books of "scripture" would become. We have recorded some of the most profound spiritual experiences in our family. Some of what I recorded is also funny. All of it is interesting.

Tonight, as I read what took place years ago, I was again delighted at the reaction of our children, ages 10, 14, and 18. (Their older brother is serving a mission in Japan.) They giggled, blushed, laughed, and punctuated the fifteen-minute-review with statements like, "I remember that," "I can't believe I did that," and "Ugh!"

I am continuously amazed at the interest the children have in that record. They often spend as much as an hour reading those notebooks. The following is a typical entry:

Date: March 6, 1978 (6:35 P.M.)

Opening Hymn: "Book of Mormon Stories"

Invocation: Scott

Fun Songs – Conducted by Alan (each person selects a favorite song and the rest of the family sings along).

Erin (age 3): "Chitty Chitty Bang Bang"

Mom: "Abba Dabba Honeymoon"

Scott (age 10): "Three Blind Mice"

Dad: "The Golden Plates"

Alan (age 7) didn't want to sing a song.

Lesson: Family Home Evening Manual #27: The Blessings of Obedience

We talked about the reasons people aren't happy. It is almost always because they are not obedient. They don't put things back where they belong. They don't get their work done. They talk disrespectfully to each other. They don't have family prayer.

We then thought of things we do in our family to keep us from being happy: not minding Mom and Dad, teasing each other, not putting our things away, not listening to each other, and Mom and Dad not listening to the children. We all decided to be more obedient this week.

(Erin sat on Dad's lap and played with the cap of Dad's fountain pen while Mom gave the lesson. Erin wanted to write with Dad's pen, but Dad wouldn't let her.)

Special Announcement: Mother announced to the children that Heavenly Father is going to send us another baby in late July or early August. Scott is glad that it will be born near his birthday in September. Alan wants a boy. Scott wants a girl. Erin wants a cookie. Dad and Mom don't care if it is a girl or a boy, but they would like the baby to be healthy.

Mom reminded the children about how it felt when Erin was in her tummy and Scott and Alan could feel her kick. Surprisingly, the children didn't seem all that excited about the news. While Mom was talking, Erin walked around the living room with a pocket calculator in her mouth.

Special Musical Number: Dad sang "The South Davis Junior High School Song." Everyone thrilled at both the beauty of the melody and the marvelous quality of Dad's voice. When the two were combined with the lyrics, the family was almost moved to tears.

Closing Hymns: "Frosty the Snowman," "The Golden Plates," and "Reverently, Quietly"

Benediction: Erin

Refreshments: Sugar cookies, which Mom and Erin made this morning. The family went into the kitchen, iced the cookies, and ate all of them. They were delicious.

The ideas and activities of this chapter are neither particularly unusual nor profound. In all likelihood, the activities reported here are duplicated thousands of times each week in the homes of Church members throughout the world. The records the families make, however, are invaluable to the people for whom they are kept. To us, those records constitute a sacred history of the most important events in our lives. And as the years pass, their value increases.[4]

18

Using Vacations
to Teach the Gospel

My son's voice cracked, and then he was quiet. He looked down at his notes, at the audience, and at his notes again. His eyes glistened, and a single tear ran down his right cheek. After what seemed like forever, he put both of his hands on the pulpit in front of him and continued:

Last summer, during our family vacation, I had the chance to visit Adam-ondi-Ahman, Far West, Winter Quarters, Independence, Liberty, Nauvoo, and Carthage. The Carthage Jail stands out as the most significant place we visited.

As soon as we arrived I started getting upset. We watched a movie about the history of the building, and as time went on I became increasingly more angry. I thought, "How dare they kill the prophet of God, the person who has done more, save Jesus only, for the salvation of men in this world, than any other man that ever lived in it." [See D&C 135:3.] As we toured the jail, all I could think about was, "This is the place where they murdered Joseph Smith."

As I entered the upper room where Joseph and Hyrum spent their last hours in mortal life with John Taylor and Willard Richards, a peaceful feeling came over me. I knew that the blood of the prophet had to be shed in order for him to seal his testimony and to complete his mission here in mortality. As I saw the blood stain of Hyrum on the floor, and as I looked out the window from which the prophet fell, I knew for sure that Joseph Smith was a prophet of God and that The Church of Jesus Christ of Latter-day Saints was true.

Many other things happened during that vacation, and the Holy Ghost bore witness to me of the truthfulness of many other things. But my most memorable moment was at the Carthage Jail when the Holy Ghost testified to me that Joseph Smith was a prophet of God.

Vacation Opportunities to Teach the Gospel

Family vacations provide unique occasions to reinforce family values and teach gospel principles. In contrast to the hectic schedules in most homes, vacations give family members the chance to spend uninterrupted, quality time together that can strengthen relationships and provide opportunities for spiritual enrichment. With proper planning, families can take advantage of the increased flexibility that vacations afford and create opportunities for family members to enjoy experiences that would otherwise be impossible. However, the creation of those opportunities must be a priority, as one mother described:

> When our children were little, my husband and I decided to carefully plan our family vacations. Since we were spending all that money on experiences, we wanted to make sure that our investment paid off in helping our children feel better about themselves and in strengthening their testimonies of the gospel. We knew that if we didn't take steps to create spiritual activities, they wouldn't happen. As a result, whenever we plan a vacation, we never take our eyes off the goals of strengthening testimonies and building family unity.

Thus, even when the thrust of the family vacation is recreational or cultural, there is ample room for spiritual experiences. Sometimes we need to do nothing more than participate in the regular worshipful activities that are a part of our normal, everyday lives. In short, we keep the commandments, regardless of where we are. A young woman reported the following about the family in which she grew up:

> When I was growing up, the only thing that was really different when we went on vacations was that we were away from home. We always had family prayer. We blessed

the food at every meal, even in restaurants. We held family home evening. We also went to church. My folks gave us a choice about attending the other Sunday meetings, but we always went to sacrament meeting. That just came with being a member of our family. We planned our activities around the Sabbath, and my folks made sure that when Sunday came, we were near an organized ward or branch. My husband and I have adopted the same attitudes in our home. No matter where we are in the world, if we are near an organized ward or branch, we attend sacrament meeting.

Attending church meetings in other places provides opportunities for children to compare how things are done in their home wards with how meetings are conducted elsewhere. They also get a first-hand experience with the universal nature of the gospel and understand the consistency with which leaders conduct church meetings. A father of three described his family's experience in the following way:

> Last Christmas we spent ten days on PoiPu Beach on the island of Kauai, Hawaii. Because we had come from the Rocky Mountains, the change in scenery was both exciting and breathtaking. We saw some of the most beautiful scenery in our lives, including an aerial view from a breathtaking helicopter ride around the island. From our front window we also had a gorgeous view of the ocean. It was an ideal location, and we are convinced that it is one of the most beautiful places on the face of the earth.
>
> However, the highlight of the trip was the sacrament meeting we attended at the Kalaheo Ward on Kauai. What impressed us most was the music. Those wonderful Polynesian people sang with a spirit that I had never experienced. For an opening hymn we sang "In Our Lovely Deseret." I had not sung that hymn for thirty-five years, and my children had never heard it. As a closing hymn, we sang "As I Have Loved You" through twice. The former has since become one of my children's favorite hymns; and we now sing both hymns in every one of our family home evenings. Every time we sing them, we are reminded of that sweet experience in the Kalaheo Ward on Kauai. It is a wonderful memory.

A mother of four children reported a similar experience when she attended a sacrament meeting with her family on one of the Pacific islands: "I will never forget the spirit that I felt in that sacrament meeting. I heard a Polynesian priest bless the sacrament and, in doing so, communicate with our Heavenly Father in a way I had never before experienced. Since that time, the sacrament prayer has taken on an entirely different meaning for me."

Unfortunately, vacation schedules sometimes make it impossible to attend church meetings in an organized ward or branch, particularly when families are camping or traveling. Nonetheless, arrangements can be made to allow for variations in schedules, and families can still have meaningful, spiritual experiences. Consider, for the example, the following comments by the father of two young boys:

> Since we knew that our camping trip would not allow us to attend church, we received permission from our bishop to hold our own sacrament meeting. Our two children were five and seven years old at the time. My wife led the music, and we sang Primary songs. The children said the opening and closing prayers, and I administered to and passed the sacrament. My wife told us some stories about the Savior, and each of us bore our testimonies. The whole meeting took no more than twenty-five minutes. The children loved it so much that they wanted to have a sacrament meeting every morning. That happened ten years ago. Today, the only thing they remember about that trip was that sacrament meeting.

Even when the primary purposes of family vacations are recreational (which is usually the case), parents can build in opportunities for children to have spiritual experiences. For instance, nearly every state and much of Canada and Mexico have important sites in Church history. With a little research, a family can incorporate visits to those sites into their itinerary. In the process of providing for spiritual dimensions in their vacations, a family is richly rewarded.

Vacations often provide great latitude to tour areas of historical significance, to attend meetings, and to participate in gospel-related activities. These experiences can create memories

155

that will continue to inspire us throughout our lives. Consider, for example, the impact of the following experience on a couple and two teenage sons:

> In January of 1985 I learned that my business would take me to several cities in Europe in June. Since I had accumulated enough miles in my airline account for several free round-trip tickets, my wife and I decided to take our seventeen- and fourteen-year-old sons with us. Predictably, the following five months were filled with a great deal of excitement and anticipation.
>
> After calling the Swiss Temple president, we arranged our schedule to coincide with the day baptisms for the dead would be performed in English. Our sons could then participate in baptismal work while we went through a temple session.
>
> Our first stop was Zollikoffen, Switzerland. After spending the night in a neighboring town, we arrived at the temple promptly at eight the next morning. The kindly temple officiators immediately took custody of our sons. While we went through an endowment session, each of them did thirty baptisms for the dead. It was a great experience for them.
>
> During the remainder of the trip we saw some of the most beautiful scenery on the face of the earth. The Swiss Alps were magnificent. The German and Austrian countryside was breathtaking. But to this day our sons maintain that the highlight of that trip was the few hours they spent at the Swiss Temple, where the Spirit of the Lord bore witness to them of the truth of the gospel and the importance of temple work. Had we not gone to the temple that day, we would never have had that experience.

It is ironic that in the above cases those who participated did not anticipate profound spiritual experiences. They were merely trying to provide opportunities for their children to grow spiritually. As they did so, the Lord blessed their efforts and provided them with rich experiences that had a profound impact on their lives. In each case, the highlight of his or her vacation was the experience with the Spirit. Children know they can have spiritual experiences at home. But providing opportunities for spiritual experiences away from home can help them understand that the gospel is universal and realize that God can bless them anywhere in the world.

THE PROCESS
OF TEACHING
THE GOSPEL
IN THE HOME

19

Teaching Children
to Resolve Problems

As I looked out the living room window, I saw my seven-year-old daughter walking up the driveway. She looked like she had been crying. I opened the front door and asked, "Good heavens, Sally, what's the matter?"

"Oh, Mommy," she said and burst into tears.

After rocking together in the rocking chair for a few minutes, I said, "Would you like to tell me what happened?"

Sally slowly nodded her head and haltingly told me the events at school that had caused so much distress. "Bobby laughed at my art and said it was dumb. Jane laughed too and said it looked awful."

"I'll bet that feels terrible." She nodded and tried to hold back the tears. We then talked at length about how she felt. The more she talked, the more intently I listened.

After she finished talking, I asked, "How are you going to handle it?"

"I don't know. I just don't know what to do."

"Would you like to know what some other children have tried?"

"Uh huh," she answered.

We talked about the various ways she could handle things and explored the possible consequences of each alternative. I then asked, "What do you think Jesus would do?"

She immediately excluded the possibilities of hitting the other children, tearing up their artwork, telling the teacher, or ignoring the problem. That left only one alternative. She said, "If anyone makes fun of my art, I'll just say, "I like my art, and I think yours is nice too." Then she added, "But what if I can't remember what to say? I'm scared."

"Why don't we ask Heavenly Father for help?" So we knelt down by her bed, and she explained her problem to Heavenly Father and asked him for help. The next morning before she went to school we again rehearsed what she would say and how she would handle it. We then knelt together in prayer, and I kissed her good-bye.

When Sally came home from the school that afternoon, she bounded into the living room and excitedly reported that it had worked exactly as we had planned. When Bobby made comments about her work, she said, "I like my art work, and I think yours is nice too." He said, "Thanks," and walked away, and nobody else said anything.

I felt thrilled that my daughter could see how Heavenly Father would help her. We went again to her bedroom and knelt in prayer, then she thanked Heavenly Father for helping her resolve this problem.

Teaching Children to Resolve Problems

One of our major responsibilities as parents is to help our children to succeed as adults. Throughout their lives they will be faced with problems. Some will be simple. Others will seem overwhelming. Problems are a part of life, and they cannot be avoided. Since the quality of our children's lives directly relates to their ability to resolve problems, we need to give them so much practice dealing with problems when they are little that, by the time they are adults, it will be second nature to them.

The most important aspect of solving problems is to rely on the Lord. That is exactly what the Prophet Joseph Smith did. After reading "If any of you lack wisdom, let him ask of God, that giveth to all men liberally, and upbraideth not; and it shall be given him" (James 1:5), Joseph took his problem to the Lord. Our children need to understand that the same process will work for them, and that they can go to the Lord at any time with any problem and get an answer to their prayers. Their Father in

Heaven is their most valuable resource. By including Heavenly Father in the problem-solving process, our children develop faith and understand better the great blessings that come from drawing close to our Father in Heaven in prayer.

Within the gospel context, then, children can apply the various steps to resolving problems. Jim Fay suggests a five-step process to help parents get their children to solve their own problems.[1] *First, we show empathy.* This lets children know that we care about them and that we understand how they're feeling. That's important, because children probably won't listen to us until they believe that we understand how they feel.

Second, we give them the implied message that they are so smart that we don't have to tell them what to do. In effect, we give them a vote of confidence and let them know they are responsible people. This can be done by simply saying, "How do you think you're going to handle it?"

Third, we get permission to share alternatives. This is done by asking a simple question: "Would you like me to tell you what other children have *tried* before?" Not *done*, but *tried*. Why this approach? Because children will listen to what other children have tried much more than to what their parents have done— or worse yet, think they *ought* to do. It also gives us permission to present some outrageous alternatives to let them know how really badly things can be handled.

Fourth, we help them see the consequences of their behavior. By predicting the impact of each suggestion one at a time, we provide them with the opportunity to anticipate the results of each alternative.

Fifth, we let children decide to solve or not solve the problem. This places the responsibility for the problem directly on their shoulders, which is where it belongs. They are the ones who have the problem, and they are the ones who must decide what to do about it.

Let's look at an example to illustrate this five-step process for helping children gain skills in solving their own problems. As we do so, we will identify each of the steps the father and daughter went through (because of the complexity of this particular example, each step was repeated twice). This experience was related by the father of a ninth-grade girl.

As I walked up the basement steps into the kitchen, I was struck by the silence. John, my eleven-year-old, who had been singing while writing his spelling words, looked sheepishly over his glasses at me and didn't make a sound. He then looked up at Karen, who was standing next to the telephone, crying.

"I hate her! I hate her so much! How could she do this to me?"

"What's the matter?"

Karen looked at me with tears running down her cheeks. "I hate her so bad!" she repeated.

I led my fifteen-year-old daughter into the living room, and the two of us sat down on the couch. "Tell me what happened."

"I just got off the phone with Mary. She told me that today, after sixth period, Nancy was really mad and said, 'I don't think Karen deserved to be elected the ninth grade's best personality. It just isn't fair. She just didn't deserve it. She also didn't deserve to make the volleyball team. She gets everything she wants, and I never get anything.' This is my best friend talking. We even live next door to each other. Nancy has been my best friend ever since the fifth grade, and now she's saying things about me behind my back. How could she do that? I'll never trust her again. I'll get her for this. Mary can't stand her and is going to tell her off tomorrow." By this time she was sobbing.

She reached out her hand. I took it and squeezed, and she continued crying. After what seemed like an eternity, I said, "I think that's awful. If my best friend said that about me, I'd feel terrible."

[*Empathy established; go to the next step.*]

"Yeah, it really hurts, Dad. I don't know what I'll do, but I'm not going to let her get away with this." I remained silent. Finally she stopped crying and asked, "Why would she do something like that? I mean, what would make her turn on me like that? You don't talk about your best friend that way."

"Well," I said slowly, "several things could have happened."

164

"Like what?"

"Well, maybe she didn't say it at all. Maybe Mary's just making it up."

"I know she said it. Sara and Tanya both told me that she's been saying things about me behind my back, but I didn't believe them. But I know that Mary wouldn't lie to me."

"Well, if you're sure that she said it, there may be several things that could explain it. Maybe she's just a hateful person."

"No! At least not before today. She's really a very kind person."

"Maybe she's jealous of you."

"Why would she be jealous of me?"

"Have you gotten anything lately that she wanted?"

"No. Well, maybe. She tried out for the volleyball team but didn't make it. She also wasn't elected to anything today, either. That could have caused it." By this time she had stopped crying.

"How are you going to handle it?"

[*You've let her know she's capable of taking care of the problem; go to the next step.*]

"I don't know. Do you have any ideas?"

"I can tell you what some other teens have tried if you'd like."

"Yeah, I'd like that."

[*You've obtained permission to share alternatives; go to the next step.*]

"Well, you could go over to her house right now, and when she comes to the door, hit her in the mouth and tell her, 'I hate you and I'll never speak to you again as long as I live.' "

"That's stupid. All she'd do is get more angry at me. Besides, that's the way children handle problems."

"If you don't like that idea, you can always do nothing. Maybe the whole thing will just go away, and you both will forget about it."

"Nope. This one isn't going to go away. I've got to do something."

165

"Well, you could wait and let some of the other kids rough her up a bit and let her know she can't treat you that way."

"That might work. But I'd be letting them do the fighting for me, and she'd think that I'm weak."

"You could also sit down with her privately and talk with her. The Lord put it this way: 'If thy brother or sister offend thee, thou shalt take him or her between him or her and thee alone; and if he or she confess thou shalt be reconciled.' [D&C 42:88.] Does that sound like it might work?"

"But what would I say to her?" Karen asked.

"You can tell her what you heard, describe how you feel about it, and explain what it's doing to your relationship."

"I've never done anything like that before. That sounds hard."

"Yeah, it would probably be tough, but I'm sure you can handle it. And if you handle it right, you'll be able to save a friendship. If you don't, you might hate each other all through high school. What do you think the Savior would do if he had a problem like this?"

"He'd probably talk to her and then forgive her. But I don't know if I can do that."

"There could be some benefit in thinking about it. You might also want to pray about it. One thing's for sure: your Father in Heaven knows what to do. Let me know if I can be of any help."

[*You've looked at the consequences and you've let her decide to solve or not solve the problem.*]

The next evening, as Karen and I sat on the living-room couch, she said, "Dad, I prayed about this last night, and I think the best way to handle this problem with Nancy is to talk to her myself. I haven't said anything to anyone about it, but everyone at school is so mad at her they could kill her."

"But I'll bet it feels good to have all of that support."

[*Empathy established; go to the next step.*]

"Yeah, it really does. But Nancy is the one I'm worried about. She's really in for a lot of trouble. I think we'd better work this out."

"How are you going to handle it?"

[*You've let her know she's capable of taking care of the problem; go to the next step.*]

"I don't know. Can you give me any ideas?"

[*You've obtained permission to share alternatives; go to the next step.*]

"Well, you can tell her you're sorry for your part in this problem."

"That's crazy. I didn't do anything."

"Okay. Another possibility is to really rip into her and tell her what a rotten friend she's been."

"That wouldn't work. All she'd do is get angry and hate me even more."

"Okay. Then you could tell her that you caught her red-handed and let her squirm."

"She would probably just get defensive and tell me she didn't do it. Then I'd have to call her a liar, and we'd get nothing solved."

"Well, one of the safest ways I know to handle problems like this is to describe the behavior by telling her what you heard, explain how you feel about it, let her know what she's doing to your relationship, and tell her what it would take to solve the problem."

"Hmm. That sounds tough, but maybe it would work. Can you give me an example?"

"Sure. What did she do?"

"She talked about me behind my back."

"Did you hear her say it?"

"No, but everybody else did."

"Well?"

"Oh, I see. So I should say, 'Some other people have told me that you've been talking behind my back.' "

"Good."

"Then what do I say?"

"Well, how did it make you feel?"

"I got really mad. But it also hurt a lot! That isn't the way best friends are supposed to treat each other."

"That's right. Tell her that."

"You mean, say those words to her?"

"It certainly would help her to understand how you feel. Next, what is her behavior doing to your relationship?"

"It's totally ruining it. I don't want her as a friend when she does that to me."

"You're right on track, so far. Now, what would you like to have her do about it?"

"I'd like her to stop talking about me behind my back. If I've done something to tick her off, I want her to tell me about it herself. I don't want to hear about it from somebody else."

"Well, it sounds as though you have at least one way of effectively handling the problem."

"Dad, can you think of anything else I should say?"

"You could tell her how important her friendship is to you. If you talk to her the way you just talked to me, I think she'll get the message and still be able to save face. You might be able to save a friendship. I'll be interested to hear how it turns out."

[*You've looked at the consequences and let her decide to solve or not solve the problem; go to the next step.*]

"I probably ought to do this before anyone else talks to her. Well, here goes." Her eyes had begun to sparkle. She got up, walked into the kitchen, and dialed Nancy's number. After the conversation, Karen described to me the phone call:

Karen: "I'd like to make an appointment for us in the counselor's office tomorrow."

Nancy: "Why?"

Karen: "Because a lot of people have told me that you've been talking about me behind my back, and I don't understand why you'd do that."

Nancy: "Oh, that's just great." (Silence.)

Karen: "All right, I'll make the appointment." Nancy then hung up.

Karen looked at me, smiled again, and said, "Now it's *our* problem. I already feel better."

Late the next afternoon, when I picked her up from volleyball practice, Karen excitedly described her meeting with Nancy in the counselor's office, shared their conversation about the problem, and summarized their agreement that if either person does anything to bug the other, she'll tell her about it.

"So how did things finally turn out?" I asked.

"We both cried and hugged each other. Now we're friends again. I felt so much in control. I knew exactly what I was doing. It was great. I never realized it could be so easy."

Thirty minutes later, as we knelt around our dinner table in family prayer, Karen said, "Heavenly Father, I'm so grateful to thee for helping me solve this problem with Nancy and that we can still be friends."

When we teach children to solve their own problems, we help them with skills they can use the rest of their lives. By including prayer in the process, they take advantage of their most valuable resource: their Father in Heaven. In the process, faith is built and testimonies are strengthened. They also come to know that regardless of their circumstances, they are never alone, and that God will hear and answer their prayers.

20

Preparing Children
for the Ordinances
of the Priesthood

It should have been a day of excitement. Terry, my son, and Billy, his best friend, were going to be baptized within the hour. But as we changed to our baptismal clothes in the dressing room, something was obviously wrong. As Billy stooped to pull on his white socks, his hand started shaking. He then stood up, turned toward the wall, and wiped a tear from his cheek.

"Is anything wrong?" I asked. Billy didn't answer. Terry walked across the dressing room, put his hand on Billy's shoulder, and asked, "Is anything the matter?"

"I guess I'm just a little scared."

"How come?" Terry asked.

" 'Cause I heard that some kids almost drown when they get baptized."

"That's crazy. Didn't anybody show you what's going to happen?"

"Nope."

"You don't need to worry. My dad's taken me through this a thousand times. You'll go into the water, and Brother Smith will take hold of your hands. After he says a prayer, and you grab your nose, he puts you under the water and pulls you out again. It'll be over in a second, and you won't even know what has happened. Here, let me show you how to do it."

Terry then held Billy's hand the same way I had held his so many times during the past month. He showed Billy how to stand, how to kneel down so his feet wouldn't pop up out of the water, and how to stand back up. Had I not reached out to catch them when they lost their balance, the two of them would have ended up in a pile on the floor.

After we stopped laughing, Terry said, "Would you like my dad to show you how to do it?" Billy nodded, so I took him by the hand and showed him exactly what he would experience, beginning with when he entered the baptismal font. We then repeated the process until he felt comfortable. After we concluded, I thought, "How unfortunate. Here we have one of the most important events in the life of this young man—his baptism into the church of Jesus Christ—and nobody has taken the time to help him understand something so simple as how to keep from drowning."

The Importance of Teaching Children about the Ordinances

The ordinances of the priesthood are central to the gospel of Jesus Christ, and they are of such significant import that only through them can we be exalted and return to live with God. Everything we do in the Church is designed to help prepare members to participate in those ordinances and to then keep the covenants they make during those sacred rites and ceremonies.

We as parents have the sacred responsibility to instill within our children a desire to participate in the priesthood ordinances and to help them prepare for those ordinances, so that the blessings and powers that the Lord wants to give them will be manifest in their lives. Specifically, children need to understand what the ordinances of the priesthood are, how and where they are performed, what the covenants are that accompany them, and why they are absolutely essential to their own eternal welfare. There are many ways we can accomplish this. For example, a mother of five described the preparation in her home in the following way:

> We have always taken seriously the Lord's commandment to prepare our children for the ordinances of the priesthood. In the case of baptism, we typically start discussing the ordinance in family home evening about six months before the child turns eight. The *Family Home Evening Resource Book* has some wonderful lessons geared to help chil-

171

dren prepare for the various ordinances, and we have found them to be enormously helpful. We read the scriptures and let them know what the Lord said about the subject. We also take our children to baptismal services so they can see what happens when people are baptized and confirmed members of the Church. In addition, we talk about it a lot around the dinner table and during our visits at bedtime. It's something the entire family looks forward to, and the closer the "big day" gets, the more excited we all become.

A father explained how he prepared his sons to receive the priesthood:

Ordinations are very important in our house. Only once, throughout all the eternities, will my sons be ordained to each office in the priesthood. Therefore, we spend a great deal of time reading the scriptures and helping them understand the covenants they'll make when they participate in the ordinances of the priesthood. We go to great lengths to explain to them exactly what they promise Heavenly Father to do *and* what he, in turn, promises he will do for them. Once they participate in the ordinance, much more is expected of them, and they must behave accordingly. The responsibility is just too great to treat lightly.

There are also some practical matters that relate to the ordinances. Daniel, our youngest son, was ordained a priest two weeks ago. Before he blessed the sacrament for the first time, I showed him where in the scriptures the prayers were located, and we talked about how meaningful it is to the Church members when the ordinance is conducted properly. He practiced the prayers several times. When he finally knelt to bless the bread for the first time, he was really nervous, but he did a marvelous job. He had a successful experience his first time up, and that is important.

Given the limited perspective of most children, particularly when they're younger, it seems unreasonable to expect them to understand all the implications of priesthood ordinances. Therefore, we need to build support systems to help reinforce the importance of what they have experienced and to instill within them the need to keep the covenants and obligations associated with those ordinances. This can be done in a variety of different ways. For example, part of this reinforcement comes automatically by participating in the normal activities and programs of the Church. One fourteen-year-old young man recounted his experience:

> For me, life really began when I was ordained a deacon. Then all kinds of things started to happen. I started attending priesthood with the older guys and adults. I got to pass the sacrament, collect fast offerings, and sometimes be the bishop's messenger. I also got to attend general priesthood meeting and see the prophet.
>
> At the same time I was ordained a deacon, I became a Scout, so I got to go to troop meetings and participate in Scout activities like hikes and campouts. I also got to go to Mutual activities and to do things I had never done before.

However, the responsibility for reinforcing the importance of ordinances lies with parents, and we can do a great deal to help our children understand that they have engaged in something very special. The father of four boys and a girl explained a unique approach that he and his wife found effective with their family:

> We try to help make the ordinance relate to as much of their lives as possible, so we schedule some very specific changes in family patterns to coincide with the years in which they are baptized and ordained to the various offices in the priesthood or advanced through the Young Women's organization.
>
> These changes often include increasing both their privileges and their responsibilities. For example, when our children get baptized, they get to select any restaurant in the city, and the whole family goes out to dinner as part of a celebration. They also get to negotiate their bedtime. The other side of it is that their responsibilities around the house also increase — not a lot, but enough to let them know that more is expected of them.
>
> When our children turn twelve, they no longer have a bedtime, and they no longer need a baby-sitter when we go out for the evening. That is a major accomplishment for

173

a twelve-year-old. But we also no longer get them up in the morning. It is their responsibility to get themselves out of bed. The boys are also expected to start wearing a coat and tie to church. They officiate in the priesthood ordinances, and they need to dress in a way consistent with that sacred responsibility.

Things continue to change as they get older. At fourteen, they get additional privileges. They also assume full responsibility for their school work, which means that we stop bugging them about doing their homework and studying for exams. When they turn sixteen, they get a set of keys to both cars; but they are also expected to pay for their own gasoline and to start picking up some of the cost for their clothes.

As is probably obvious by now, we have found that the most effective way to reinforce the importance of priesthood ordinances is to tie them to something tangible. These changes don't substitute for teaching them the gospel; they just add meaning to the importance of the ordinance. It helps them to understand that being baptized and being ordained to an office in the priesthood are privileges.

Successful parents can use a variety of different ways to help their children understand the sacred nature of priesthood ordinances. Regardless of the method, however, children also need to understand that participation in priesthood ordinances also brings with it a sacred responsibility. A recently married young man described how his own father taught him about one of the sacred responsibilities associated with receiving the Aaronic Priesthood:

> When I was eleven, my dad told us in family home evening about an experience he had shortly after I was born. Sister Hanks, a member of his ward, had cancer. She had been bedridden for months, and she knew she was dying. More than anything else she desperately wanted to see her son grow to manhood. One night, at her request, her bishop gave her a blessing; and during that blessing the Spirit prompted him to promise her that she would live long enough to see her son become a man.

174

At the time Dad was teaching Course 11 in Sunday School. Her son was in his class, so he knew the family well, and he knew about that blessing. On the Sunday after the boy turned twelve, my dad, the bishop, and the entire Sunday School class met together in Sister Hanks's bedroom so she could witness her son's ordination to the office of deacon. A few days later she passed away.

Dad said that some people would question the bishop's inspiration when he promised her that she would see her son grow to be a man. Dad, however, was convinced that the prophecy the bishop made in his blessing was literally fulfilled. Dad said that when a boy receives the priesthood, he becomes a man in the Lord's eyes. That means that there is much more expected of him than before.

That story had a profound impact on my life. Dad told me that when I was given the Aaronic Priesthood, Heavenly Father thought of me as a man, and he expected me to act accordingly. I knew, for example, that the Lord expected me to help my brothers and sisters be happy and successful, and that meant I had to stop teasing and picking on them. I also knew that when my Dad left on a business trip, I had a responsibility to help take care of my mother and the rest of the family. Therefore, I did the best I could to live up to those expectations, and in the process I developed a great respect and love for the priesthood and for the power that Heavenly Father had given me.

We can also help our children understand the power of the priesthood by sharing examples and personal experiences from our own lives and from the lives of others. For example, the following story has played a significant role in helping many families understand the sacred nature of the priesthood and the protection it can provide:

> Since the island of Tutuila in American Samoa is extremely mountainous, the villages are built by the sea shore. Prior to 1980, the village of Amanave, on the western shore of the island, had not had missionaries for several years. However, due to the efforts of Vialua Lameco, one of the few members of the Church in the village, the area was

175

reopened for missionary work in the fall of 1980. Brother and Sister Lameco invited the new missionaries (Joseph Harris, from Idaho Falls, and Misiona Tuimaseve, a native Samoan from the island of Savai'i in Western Samoa) to live with their family.

The Lameco home, like the others in the village, had no walls. The tin roof was supported by posts, and the floor was made up of small pieces of rounded coral. For protection against the rain and wind, the family lowered curtains made of coconut thatch. Since the homes had no electricity, oil and gas lanterns were the only source of light at night.

Once the missionaries arrived, the Lameco family knelt together, and by the power of the priesthood Brother Lameco dedicated their home for missionary service. Although the home was humble in terms of worldly standards, it was a very sacred place.

During the month of October it rained constantly for three weeks. As a result the entire island was saturated with moisture. At four A.M. on October 28, 1980, an earthquake hit the island. The mountain above the village shifted, causing a mud slide that carried with it huge boulders that crushed and buried everything in its path.

The missionaries and the Lameco family were awakened by the earthquake. With Elder Harris's powerful gas lantern, they could see everything that was taking place within one hundred feet of their home. They first watched the torrents of water descend from the mountain and pass through the village. Within a few minutes, the water turned to mud, and then a four-foot wall of mud descended upon the village, crushing everything in its path, including trees and houses. The noise was almost deafening.

Then a miracle happened. The wall of mud came within two inches of the Lameco home, divided, completely encircled the house, joined together on the other side, and proceeded through the village, wiping out everything else in its path. The mud slide lasted for about one hour, but the Lameco home was untouched; the only evidence that anything had happened was a six-inch wall of mud two inches from the foundation. Almost everything else in the village of Amanave was destroyed.[1]

Most experiences are not this miraculous. But powerful lessons can be learned when parents bear testimony of the importance of the priesthood in their lives and provide opportunities for their children to witness the power of the priesthood ordinances. With tears running down his cheeks, a grandfather shared the following experience with the members of his ward as he bore testimony about the importance of teaching children the gospel:

> My daughter had very poor health when she was expecting her second child. One day she asked her husband and brother to give her a blessing. While they laid their hands upon her head and officiated in an ordinance of the priesthood that we prize so highly, Spencer, her energetic and inquisitive two-year-old son, sat on the couch and watched the proceedings from beginning to end without moving a muscle or making a peep! He was all eyes and ears. It was as if he fully understood the sacredness of that special occasion.
>
> Several days later his mother was having a particularly difficult day. Early that afternoon she lay down on the couch and closed her eyes, all the while listening to Spencer play. He clearly understood that his mother was ill because she had told him on several occasions that they could not do this or that because "Mommy didn't feel good."
>
> As she lay on the couch, she heard Spencer approach her and felt him standing near her. He laid his hands upon her head and said, "My mommy is sick." He then went on at length to bless her in a language comprehensible only to his Father in Heaven. While she pretended to be asleep, she shed tears of happiness for a child who, while in his infancy, was learning the ways of the Savior.

When the importance of priesthood ordinances is properly taught to our children, the lessons often create a desire in their hearts and motivate them to live worthy to receive those wonderful blessings. Sometimes, however, our teaching has a far greater impact on our children than we had ever imagined, as one mother explained:

> We had the privilege of participating in the building of

177

the Ogden Temple, and every member of our family made his or her financial contribution. We also talked about the temple and helped our children understand the kinds of things that go on in that sacred house and what a great blessing it is to be worthy to enter it and to receive the blessings the Lord has in store for us there.

Prior to leaving our home to take the tour of the temple before it was dedicated, my husband said, "Today we will stand together, as a family, in the celestial room of the temple. Pay careful attention to what you see and how you feel, because this will be the last time it will happen until each of you earns the right to be there. The only way we will be there together again is if each of you lives worthy to receive your endowments. This time it is for free. The next time you must earn the right to be there."

I'll never forget walking into the celestial room when we took our fifth child through the temple for his endowments. As our son stood there with the rest of the family, he looked at me and said, "Mom, I made it."

"What do you mean?"

"When we went through the temple before it was dedicated, Dad said that the next time we stood together in the celestial room, we had to earn the right to be here. I did it. I am worthy!"

To the best of my recollection, we had never talked about that experience; but it had such an impact on my son that thirteen years later he remembered it, word for word. We had set the stage prior to taking a tour of that wonderful building, and he had never forgotten it. Our son watched all of his brothers and sisters go through the temple. He was the last, and he made it. So again we were able to meet together in the celestial room of the temple because every one of them had earned the right to be there.

The very purpose of teaching the gospel in the home is to help our children understand gospel principles and to so live that they are worthy to participate in the priesthood ordinances. When gospel principles are taught with the companionship of the Spirit, they are embedded in the hearts and souls of those whom we teach. The impact of such teaching is profound.

178

21

Teaching Children Responsibility

It seemed hopeless. I had lectured, begged, pleaded, threat-
ened, and coerced. But nothing had worked. The harder I tried
to teach my ten-year-old responsibility, the more he resisted. I
was getting nowhere, and I was making myself miserable in the
process.

One afternoon my Relief Society visiting teacher shared a few
pages from a book she had recently read. One particular passage
struck me as the perfect answer:

> *I've got a friend who says she lends money to her kids. She's*
> *"Mom, the bank" at her house. She says she's just like the First*
> *National Bank, handing out money all the time. But she loves to*
> *do it because she does it just like the First National Bank—she*
> *requires promissory notes and collateral. Her kids always know*
> *when they're going to pay the loans back and what the collateral*
> *is. Once, for example, she repossessed a $29.00 tape recorder from*
> *her son. And I think her son was fortunate. Here he was—ten*
> *years old, and he learned all about banks and responsibility and*
> *collateral and repossessions. And all it cost him was a $29.00 tape*
> *recorder. Some people protect their kids, and the kids don't get to*
> *learn that lesson until they're 35, and somebody repossesses their*
> *$29,000 car.*[1]

I was amazed at how simple it was. I had consistently pro-
tected my son from the real world and then become frustrated
because he wasn't learning to be responsible. By denying him the
opportunities to make mistakes, I was, in fact, preventing him

from the growth and development that come from experiencing the consequences of his behavior.

Teaching Children Responsibility

Teaching children responsibility means teaching them to be honest, dependable, and trustworthy. It also means helping them learn to make decisions and to then live with the natural consequences of their behavior. Unfortunately, helping our children to become responsible adults is almost always harder on us than it is on them, primarily because the natural consequences of behavior are often uncomfortable and occasionally painful; and we don't like to see our children experience pain.

Teaching children to be responsible is also no small task. In fact, most parents really don't understand for sure how to do it. As a father of seven children explained:

> As far as I'm concerned, I can't tell you for sure how we teach our children to be responsible. Responsibility is something they have to learn for themselves. We can provide opportunities for them to learn, but they have to tough it out and learn the valuable lessons of life themselves. Responsibility can only be learned by experience. Therefore, one of the most important things we can do for children is to allow them to have the kinds of experiences that will prepare them for life. That means that we have to be willing to let them make mistakes and to then learn from the consequences.

Children who are protected from the consequences of their actions are not prepared to succeed in the real world. Fortunately, however, the real-world lessons of life can be learned much more inexpensively in our homes, when children are young.

A variety of things contribute to rearing responsible children, one of which is a clear set of family rules. Rules are essential to successful family life. They establish guidelines, state values, and define the limits of acceptable behavior. Parents who base all family decisions on the results of an applause meter are begging for serious trouble. On some issues we need to take an unwavering stand, regardless of the popularity of the decision. However, most issues aren't that black and white. Thus, a clear set of rules serves as a practical framework that children can rely on to help them set standards, make decisions, and resolve problems. Rules also help children understand family values and provide them with an anchor as they grow and develop.

Generally speaking, the fewer the number of formal rules, the better, as long as they are clearly understood and accepted by family members and are broad enough to provide the necessary guidelines for family living. As a father of five teenagers explained:

> Although we don't spend a lot of time talking about it, we expect family members to live Church standards, treat our home with respect, and do their chores. As far as specific, formal rules are concerned, we have only three. First, we don't say or do anything that will undermine another family member's self-esteem.
>
> Second, whenever we leave home, we tell someone (for children, it means one of the parents) where we are going, whom we will be with, and when we will return. If plans change, we notify the family by telephone so people will know when to expect us. The children will also let us know when they have arrived home, regardless of the hour.
>
> Third, we will be where we are supposed to be when we are supposed to be there. In short, we are expected to be dependable.
>
> We agreed as a family that everyone lives by the same set of rules, parents and children alike. No exceptions. These simple rules are fair to everyone, yet they are broad enough to set a standard for our behavior. We have found few problems that cannot be addressed by adhering to these three rules. But we expect everyone to keep them, and we do whatever is necessary to insure that we all live by the same set of standards.[2]

Chores also provide excellent opportunities for children to learn responsibility. They help children understand that they have to work for what they get, and regularly fulfilling their responsibilities also helps them learn to work. As one father explained:

181

As I was growing up, my father was in the construction business, so I learned to work at his side. I worked full time during the summer and after school and on Saturdays during the school year. My children aren't so fortunate. I am in an office all day, so I can't work with my children. That is why chores are so important. They help my children learn to work. They also help teach them that they need to work for what they get. Helping with the load is part of the cost of living with someone.

The children in our house start doing chores when they are old enough to walk. For example, our two-year-old picks up his toys, puts his clothes away, and makes sure the bathroom towels and washcloths are hung up. When he does a good job, we tell him about it. If he needs help, we provide it. As he gets older, he will have more responsibility; and we don't do things for him that he can do for himself. Given my work life, this is about the only way we have to teach our children to work.

Chores can be assigned in a variety of different ways. A mother of three teenagers described how chores get handled in her home:

> Most of the time we let our children choose what they want to do from a list of things that need to be done. We handle the things we don't like to do in two ways: we either rotate them through the family on a periodic basis, or we do them together. The weekly chores are to be completed no later than 4:30 P.M. on Saturday. Since our older children like to do things on Saturday night, the deadline provides a motivation for them, since getting chores done is a prerequisite to using the family car.

Regardless of our method of assigning chores, we need to follow through and make certain that our children fulfill their responsibilities. That is not always easy, particularly as the children get older. A practical mother of three children gave the following insight.

> I give my children a responsibility, and then I hope that they make a mistake. Why? Because they will then learn

something from it—and they will learn it at the cheapest possible price. I would much rather have my son learn to be responsible at age six than at sixteen or twenty-six. If he's supposed to vacuum the living room by the end of the day, I don't feel the least bit guilty about awakening him out of a deep sleep to complete his chores. That way he knows we mean business, he learns a valuable lesson about being dependable, and the living room gets vacuumed. Incidentally, I have never had to do something like that more than once with each of my children. It's amazing how responsible they become when they know we mean business. As long as it's done with love, we don't damage our relationship with our children.

Expecting children to behave responsibly prepares children for the real world, and that is what parenting is all about. Typically, the more practical the example, the richer the learning experience. A father of four described an important lesson that he learned in a simple way:

> As I sat at our kitchen table, Mom took two dishes from the refrigerator and set one in front of me and one in front of my little sister.
> "What's that?" I asked.
> "It's lemon pudding—the kind of stuff that seven-year-old boys like you really enjoy."
> "What's it taste like?"
> "Try it and see," she said, smiling.
> "It looks awful. I hate that stuff."
> Mom smiled at me even more and said, "Oh, really? Well, that's okay, Jimmy, you don't have to eat it." She then promptly put my dish back in the refrigerator.
> "Hey, I was just kidding."
> "I don't mind. I'll just give it to one of your sisters."
> "Mom!"
> "I really don't mind. Some people just aren't cut out for lemon pudding."
> "What am I going to have for dessert?"
> "Don't know. Maybe some peanut butter and honey on a slice of bread."

183

"I don't want peanut butter and honey!" My four-year-old sister looked over her half-eaten dish of pudding and said, "Jimmy, dat was weally dumb ta say dat. Dis stuff is weally good."

Even though that incident took place forty years ago, I remember it as if it happened yesterday. It's amazing to me that such a simple event could help me to understand the implications of making judgments without accurate information. That was certainly the last time I ever turned up my nose at dessert before I tasted it. And since that time I've been very careful about jumping to conclusions without having all of the facts.

In the process of holding children accountable, we need to make it absolutely clear that we love them and that we care for them. That's why empathy and concern are so important. In fact, one of the worst possible things we can say to our children when we try to teach them to solve their own problems is "This is your problem," or "It's not my problem." It's much better to imply it by saying, "Well, that must feel pretty rotten," or "That's a real bummer," or some other phrase that lets them know that we care about them and that we understand their difficulty.[3] A sixteen-year-old girl described how her father got that message across and still held her accountable:

> We have a rule in our house that we can't drive the family car until we have completed a driver's education course. My two older brothers had adhered to the rules, and I was expected to do the same. Since the subject wasn't taught in our high school, Dad paid for the lessons. But we had to enroll in the course.
>
> On my sixteenth birthday, my friend took me down to get my driver's license. However, it did me no good, because my folks wouldn't let me behind the wheel until I got the training; and I hadn't bothered to sign up.
>
> Six weeks after turning sixteen, I enrolled in an intensive course — one where I could get the class and the eight hours of driving in a two-week period. Halfway through the second week, I got in a jam and needed to use the car. Dad refused.

"But Daddy," I pleaded, "I have only two more hours of driving, and then the class will be over."

He put his arms around me, hugged me, and said, "Sweetheart, I know it's a bummer not to be able to drive. I'm willing to take you where you need to go. But if I were to let you take the car after all I've said about this subject, you would never be able to really trust me again." He then kissed me, told me how much he loved me, and left me alone to solve my problem. How could you not love a guy like that?

Unfortunately, not all problems can be handled so easily, particularly when children get older. For example, what about stubborn teenagers. What if they refuse to do their chores? What do you do if your sixteen-year-old son refuses to do what you ask? There may be times when the following approach may be helpful:

If he refuses to do what I ask, I say to him, "Did I ask you in a nice way?"

"Yes," he'll say, "you asked me in a nice way."

"I asked you in a nice way, and you're still not going to do it? Hey, no problem. I'll do it myself," I reply.

And I do. I do it myself, and I don't make an issue of it whatsoever, but I don't forget.

Now maybe the next day the boy comes to me and he needs me. I don't know a kid alive who isn't going to need me as a parent. He says, "Hey, remember, this is Saturday. And you were going to take me out for a driving lesson."

I say, "Oh, yeah, I remember that, Pal. And you're even asking me in a nice way. But, rats! Guess what I learned last night—from you, by the way? I learned that asking in a nice way around this house just doesn't cut it. Try me again another time. I mean don't give up on me."

Or another technique I suggest to handle this big kid I can't overpower is to keep track of the time it takes to do the chore he won't do. Then when he comes to me on Saturday and asks if he can have a driving lesson, I say, "Well, probably so, except that I used up that time raking the leaves for you, so why don't you check back with me when I haven't used up the time."[4]

185

We need to remember that teaching children responsibility involves a step-by-step process that takes years to accomplish. "All that's required is a consistent effort by patient, loving parents who respect their children too much to let them be infantile when they are ready to be nearly adult."[5]

22

Teaching Missionaries

I opened the mailbox, and facing me from the top of the stack of bills sat that much-waited-for brown envelope containing a letter from our missionary son. I tore it open and hungrily read the almost illegible handwriting:

> *Dear Mom and Dad,*
> *Thanks for your recent letter. I can't tell you how much it meant to me. You have no idea what I've been going through. I was beginning to believe all the negative stuff I've been hearing from those gentiles, and a week of having doors slammed in my face was really getting to me. When you told me about how the Lord had answered your prayers when Dad was sick and then bore your testimony to me about the importance of the work I am doing, I really felt the Spirit. It was awesome. I can't tell you how much better it made me feel. I love you dearly and am so grateful that you are my parents. Please keep the letters coming.*

Could this be my *son? I couldn't believe what I was reading. Before he left on his mission, he wouldn't give me the time of day. I had no idea what a positive impact a simple letter would have on his life. He isn't even the same boy.*

Can We Really Teach Missionaries?

At first thought, the idea of teaching the gospel to our missionary children seems mildly absurd. In fact, we have heard some people argue just the opposite:

We have spent a lifetime teaching them the gospel and preparing them to serve missions. Now we have sent them out to teach the gospel, not to be taught. Our role, as parents, is to encourage, to support, to sustain them financially and with our love. They are in the Lord's hands, and there is really very little we can do to teach them the gospel. Besides, we don't know anything about missionary work, anyway. Our job in that area stopped when they walked through the doors of the Missionary Training Center!

However, the above perceptions could not be further from the truth. Consider, for example, the following observation by a father of two returned missionaries:

When my oldest son received his call from the prophet, there was nothing in that letter that released me from my responsibility as his father. Even though he is on the Lord's errand, he is still my son, and I have a sacred obligation to do all that I can to help him be successful in all of his righteous endeavors. The Lord's commandment to teach our children the gospel did not include the phrase "except while they are serving missions." In fact, I have come to understand that my opportunity to teach him is far greater now than it has been in years.

There are few times in our children's lives when they are so receptive to learning the truths of the restored gospel as when they are in the mission field. They spend one hundred percent of their time engaged in that great service. They are immersed in learning and teaching the principles of the gospel. The more we can help them with that difficult task, the more successful they will be.

A common barrier to teaching our children is their disinterest in what we have to say. In fact, one of the major reasons we are commanded to teach our children the gospel before the age of eight is that those are the years when they believe what we tell them. They have the childlike faith that God commanded all of us to have, and Satan has no power to tempt them. (See D&C 29:47.) The family is still far more influential than the peer group.

However, as they get older, their attitudes often start to

change. They begin to question our judgment, particularly when they see inconsistencies between what we teach and the ways we sometimes behave. It is not surprising, then, that they become more skeptical and sometimes cynical.

The only time they approach that same childlike level of receptivity again is in the mission field. Their full-time jobs are to teach the principles of the gospel, and they are hungry for anything that will help them better accomplish that task. Their success as missionaries depends upon it. The father of four missionaries shared the following observations:

Shortly after our eldest son entered the Missionary Training Center, I realized that I had been granted, rather miraculously, a fresh opportunity to be his teacher. In his early years I had done much of that, but as his horizons had expanded, he had seemed to pay less and less attention to me, until there were times when I felt like an outsider in his life.

But now, in the midst of his commitment to serve the Lord on a mission, our son for the first time in his life discovered that he missed us. He was not necessarily homesick, but at least he missed us. And as all missionaries know, missing their families is best cured by letters from home.

Also understanding that, I sent those letters diligently. And only gradually did I come to the realization that my son was again a "captive" audience. No matter what I wrote, in his desperation for contact with home, he would read and even reread it, often many times.

From there it was an easy jump to including in my letters small lessons that I was learning or had learned, things that I thought might help him. These weren't major things but were usually items I had gleaned from family or personal scripture study, or personal experiences that seemed designed by a loving Heavenly Father to help me view one concept or another from an eternal perspective.

Then came a letter from our missionary telling of a problem or a situation and actually asking for counsel. I responded joyfully but carefully, using the scriptures as a guide, and I was gratified to see the counsel accepted. More

189

letters came, more questions were asked, sometimes even about gospel topics, and more and more I found myself studying the gospel and writing letters with a new purpose — to locate and share gospel gemstones that would help our son find success in his labors for Christ.

A year passed and our second son departed for his mission, and three months later our daughter entered the MTC for her own mission experience. And within a month or so of her departure, my wife and I noticed an amazing coincidence. The letters from our newest missionaries were almost exact parallels of the earlier letters from our eldest elder, both in experiences shared and in questions asked. And all three were serving in widely separated locations around the earth, laboring within vastly divergent cultures.

Now, with three children home from their missions, and a fourth serving and again writing parallel letters, I am convinced of the tremendous opportunities parents have to teach their children the gospel.[1]

This need to be spiritually fed has clear implications for what and how we communicate to our missionaries. Since letters are our only means for communicating with them, we need to exercise care in what we write. Letters containing criticism, complaints, and detailed descriptions of personal and family problems do not lift and motivate. As one missionary explained, "Letters from home are wonderful if they are newsy and positive. But it's difficult when I get a letter out here from my family members, and they talk about all the problems they're having. It's frustrating because I can't help. I can't do a single thing about it except wring my hands and worry. I hate getting those kinds of letters. Quite frankly, there are some things that I just don't want to know about right now."

On the other hand, letters that contain encouragement, statements of support, and detailed descriptions of successful experiences give uplifting and inspiring messages. Sharing spiritual experiences, reporting family members' accomplishments, quoting relevant scriptures, and bearing our testimonies can build faith and motivate our children in ways that cannot be

190

duplicated by anyone else. We can teach them gospel principles and motivate them to the point that when they finish reading our letters, they feel uplifted, inspired, and more committed to building the kingdom. Never underestimate the influence of letters from home. Consider, for example, the impact of a letter about the importance of obedience:

> It was great to get your letter this week. Dad, your letter has me so excited to work hard. That has got to be one of the most inspired letters you have ever written to me. So far I've read it twenty times, and I'm still excited every time I read it. I never really understood the relationship between obedience and the Lord blessing me in this work. Your letters are always such a strength to me. They always make me feel so good and strengthen my resolve to do my best. I love them. If I have a choice between getting a package of goodies from home and getting a letter, I'll take a letter any day.

A mother once told her missionary son about a spiritual experience the family had in dealing with a problem facing his younger brother. After describing the experience in detail, she assured him that all of the family members felt the same level of love and support for him as well. He described the impact of that letter to his uncle in the following way:

> I just received the letter from mom telling me of the wonderful experience they had, how the family fasted and prayed together, and it was beautiful. The spirit that came from the letter was incredible, and I could not hold back the tears. Every time I read it, I am impressed at how much they love me, and how blessed I am to be a member of that family. There is no way I can fail with the support they have for me and the number of prayers that are being said for me every day.

Similar letters are sent thousands of times every week from grateful elders and sisters who are strengthened by messages of support and encouragement from their loved ones. However, the opportunity to bless missionaries is not restricted only to our children. A significant percentage of the missionary force of the Church is made up of married couples who have the same needs for support, love, and encouragement as their younger colleagues. As one father explained to his daughter:

> I look forward to your letters more than you can imagine. They are very important to me. I see them as gestures of love on your part, and I feel very encouraged by them. They are an indication of your love for us. I think they are great. They show us that you trust us and have confidence that we can do the job we have been called to do. Most of the time you have much more confidence in us than we have in ourselves.
>
> I love to hear about your feelings, your hopes, and the things you are interested in. I feel strengthened when you tell us about your prayers, and how they are answered. It is a wonderful feeling to know that we are loved and honored by those we love the most.
>
> Most people don't realize that couples who go on missions need support and encouragement as much as the younger missionaries do. I don't think there has ever been a time in my life that I have needed to hear from my family and friends as much as I do now, even if it's only just half a page. The length is not nearly as important as the frequency. I would much rather have four short letters each month than one long one.
>
> There are a lot of wonderful things about missionary work. But it gets very lonely sometimes. Letters are a great way of letting me know that I am supported.

Letters to all missionaries, whether they are single or married couples, provide unique opportunities for us to share warm expressions of the heart—those messages of love and appreciation that sometimes are awkward when we are talking face to face. For many people, some things are just easier to say in letters. Clearly, regular, positive letters have an impact on missionaries in ways that cannot be duplicated. We can do things for our missionaries that no one else can do, including teaching them gospel principles.

23

When Children Rebel

"That's what you think," I said angrily to my twelve-year-old son. "You're going inside with me, even if I have to drag you by your ear." I jumped out of the car, walked to the other side, and reached for the car door. It wouldn't open. Danny had locked himself inside, and my keys were still in the ignition. I was so angry at that kid that I was ready to string him up. At that point, I had a decision to make. I could create a scene in the church parking lot, or I could go to sacrament meeting. Since I hate to fight battles I know I can't win, I chose the latter.

Danny had resisted going to church ever since we moved to town three months ago. This morning, when he told me he wasn't going, we had a pretty heated argument. Finally, in response to my threats, he reluctantly put on his Sunday clothes and got in the car. In retrospect, I really should have known better than to push him like that. My own fears and frustrations had gotten in the way of helping my son. The more I leaned on him, the more defiant he became.

I heard little that was said in sacrament meeting. I spent the entire time praying for help on how to resolve the problem with my son. Since it made no sense to let him sit in the car for three hours, particularly since I was not getting anything out of the meeting anyway, I skipped Sunday School and Relief Society.

Fortunately, I kept my mouth shut during the ride home. Once inside the house, however, Danny went straight to his room and closed the door. My announcement an hour later that dinner

193

was ready was met with silence. I found him lying on his bed, looking at the ceiling.

"Son, I'm sorry about the way I treated you this morning. My behavior was uncalled for. I will try to never let that happen again. If you would like to talk about it, I'll be in the living room. I'll fix you a plate and put it in the oven so it'll stay warm until you're ready to eat." He continued to stare at the ceiling, and I walked out of the room.

Ninety minutes later he came into the living room and sat down on the sofa. "Thanks for dinner," he said quietly, looking at the floor.

"You're welcome. Hey, I'm really sorry about this morning. I'm sure you had a good reason for not wanting to go to church. The problem was that I didn't want to listen to you. Now I'm ready to listen."

Tears came to his eyes, and he said haltingly, "The kids at church make fun of me because of my teeth." He then started to cry. I felt sick inside. How could I have been so insensitive? He had complained for several months about how his two front teeth stuck out, but I had paid little attention to his concerns. What I had seen as rebellion against the Church was not really rebellion at all. He simply didn't want to be embarrassed again by the criticism of the other deacons.

When Children Rebel

The most effective way to prevent rebellion is to teach our children the gospel when they are young. A strong testimony provides the armor they need to withstand the influence of Satan. Children gain testimonies by learning the gospel and by having the Holy Ghost bear witness to them that what they have been taught is true. Many problems will be prevented when children *know* that Jesus is the Christ, that Joseph Smith is a prophet, and that the restored gospel is true. However, children also have their free agency. And sometimes they choose to exercise that agency in ways that are inconsistent with gospel principles.

An important step in dealing with rebellious children is to understand that rebellion is *always* a power struggle, whether the child is two, fifteen, or forty. They are rebelling against something or someone. Understandably, then, authoritarian and coercive behavior on our part only alienates and offends them. Coercion is not part of the gospel plan, and it plays no useful role in teaching the gospel to our children. Thus, when dealing with rebellious children, our teaching needs to be characterized "by persuasion, by long-suffering, by gentleness and meekness, and by love unfeigned; by kindness, and pure knowledge, which shall greatly enlarge the soul without hypocrisy, and without guile." (D&C 121:41–42.) Such an approach can work miracles. Consider, for example, the insight gained by a seventeen-year-old boy.

> For several months I was inactive in the Church. However, during that entire time my parents never leaned on me. There was no badgering and no criticism. They allowed me to exercise my free agency and then respected my choices. They loved me. They continued to teach me as often as I would listen. They forgave me when I offended them. They prayed for me. But most of all, they loved me. Therefore, I had nothing to rebel against. Throughout it all I knew that they were genuinely concerned about my welfare. As a result, it was much easier for me to come back home and to come back to church.

Another important step in helping rebellious children is to identify what they are rebelling against. Put in medical terms, we always do a diagnosis before we prescribe treatment. Once we identify the cause of the problem, we can then generate acceptable alternative solutions, and the difficulties become much more manageable. A mother of five shared the following information about her fourth child.

> Todd was a very determined young man, and during his early teenage years his strong-willed nature led him places he should not have gone. At first we thought he was rebelling against the standards he had been taught. But then we realized that he needed his freedom and independence, and he was determined to have it. We knew that our son could channel that determination into rebelling against us, or he could channel it in a more productive and

positive direction. If we had fought him, I'm afraid he would have gone the other way. He would have had something to rebel against. Teenage rebellion is a power struggle. The only way you win is not to play the game. Fortunately, we gave him the freedom he needed, and he chose to keep the commandments.

However, in spite of our best efforts, children sometimes make poor decisions. When that happens, we must not let the unwise use of their agency prevent us from keeping the commandments. A single mother reported the following:

Shortly after my son turned fifteen, his church attendance dropped off. Then one day he announced that he didn't have a testimony, and he demanded that we stop reading the scriptures, having family prayer, and holding family home evening. Stunned though I was, I explained that regardless of how he felt, we intended to live the gospel. That meant that his thirteen-year-old sister and I would continue to kneel in family prayer each evening before dinner and to read the scriptures together after we finished eating. We would also hold family home evening every Monday night. He didn't have to join us in any of those activities. But they would be held, just the same.

Heartbroken though I was, I realized that the only chance I had to reach my son was to live in such a way that I was worthy to have the companionship of the Holy Ghost. I tried to make his time at home as pleasant as possible, and I continued to love him and, at the same time, respect his wishes. But not once during the following four years did my son join us in family prayer, and he consistently evaporated as soon as we pulled out our scriptures. He attended family home evening only five times, and those were holiday celebrations. To stand back and watch him make other unwise choices was almost more than I could bear.

Then last week he joined us in reading the scriptures. The next day he asked if I thought it would be possible for him to serve a mission. When I asked him what caused the change, he said, "You've continued to love and respect me despite my mistakes. You've also stuck to your guns, as

196

far as the gospel is concerned, and your life is a lot better than mine. I've tried it my way, and it doesn't work very well. I think I'd like to try it your way for a while."

God has given all of his children their agency. In the process of choosing, mistakes will take place. Children will disappoint us. They will slip. They will be clumsy. They will sometimes do less than their best. That is part of mortality. Hence, we need to understand that our children's mistakes often say more about the poor judgment of the child than about the inadequacies of their parents.

Although teaching children the gospel is necessary for the salvation of both the parent and the child, it is not the only variable affecting the child's behavior. Other factors come into play, including the character traits and attributes they developed before they came to mortality. Not surprisingly, then, children reared in the same family can be quite different. In considering the differences among children, President Joseph F. Smith teaches us a valuable lesson about the impact of the premortal soul on our tendency to accept divine gospel truths while in mortality. Specifically, President Smith said:

> Notwithstanding this fact that our recollection of former things was taken away, the character of our lives in the spirit world has much to do with our disposition, desires and mentality here in mortal life. This spirit influences the body to a great extent, just as the body in its desires and cravings has an influence on the spirit. . . . Environment and many other causes, however, have great influence on the progress and destiny of man, but we must not lose sight of the fact that the characteristics of the spirit which were developed through many ages of the former existence play a very important part in our progression through mortal life.[1]

Despite our best efforts, children sometimes make choices that are inconsistent with gospel principles. Elder Orson F. Whitney gave the following comforting counsel to parents with wayward children:

> The Prophet Joseph Smith declared — and he never

taught more comforting doctrine – that the eternal sealings of faithful parents and the divine promises made to them for valiant service in the Cause of Truth, would save not only themselves, but likewise their posterity. Though some of the sheep may wander, the eye of the Shepherd is upon them, and sooner or later they will feel the tentacles of Divine Providence reaching out after them and drawing them back to the fold. Either in this life or the life to come, they will return. They will have to pay their debt to justice; they will suffer for their sins; and may tread a thorny path; but if it leads them at last, like a penitent Prodigal, to a loving and forgiving father's heart and home, the painful experience will not have been in vain. Pray for your careless and disobedient children; hold on to them with your faith. Hope on, trust on, till you see the salvation of God.

Who are these straying sheep – these wayward sons and daughters? They are children of the Covenant, heirs to the promises, and have received, if baptized, the Gift of the Holy Ghost, which makes manifest the things of God. Could all that go for naught?[2]

The severe pain caused by a wayward child can only be understood by one who has experienced it. As a result, many silently suffer for years because of the heartbreak and helplessness they feel. However, we can still do something for them. We can love them, and we can pray for them. President Gordon B. Hinckley provided the following insightful counsel to parents under such circumstances.

It is very easy to say that if we will do this or that, all will go well. But I have seen conscientious men and women, people who are faithful and true, people who try to observe the teachings of the Church, who still experience broken hearts over the conduct of their children.

I know some of the answers to these problems, but I confess that I do not know all of them. Many of the problems are of our own making. In other cases, they seem to happen notwithstanding all that we do to guard against them. I think of some wonderful people I know. Their older children grew up and were married and went forward with their lives in a way that made the hearts of their parents glad. And then there was a younger son, a bright and able boy. It was the associations he had in high school that moved him in another direction. His hair grew long and his dress unkempt. He did other things which brought great distress to his father and mother. His father was distraught. He scolded and threatened; he wept and prayed and rebuked his son. But there was no response. The boy went his wayward course. His mother also wept and prayed. But she controlled her feelings and kept her voice low. She repeatedly expressed to her son her love for him. He left home. She kept his room tidy, his bed made, food for him in the refrigerator, and she told him that whenever he felt like coming home, he would be made welcome.

Months passed while hearts ached.

The love of his mother finally began to touch his heart. He came back occasionally to sleep. Without ever scolding, she smiled, joked with him, placed delicious food before him, put her arms around him, and expressed her love. Finally, he began to show increasing neatness in his person. He stayed home more. He came to realize that there was no other place as comfortable, no place as secure, no place as happy as that home which he had earlier left. He finally got his life under control. He went on a mission, at an age older than most young men do. He proved to be a successful missionary. He returned home, entered school, and began to apply himself. The last time I saw him, he and his mother, each blessed with a good voice, sang a duet while some who knew the history of that family shed tears.

To any within the sound of my voice who may have such sons or daughters, may I suggest that you never quit trying. They are never lost until you have given up. Remember that it is love, more than any other thing, that will bring them back. Punishment is not likely to do it. Reprimands without love will not accomplish it. Patience, expressions of appreciation, and that strange and remarkable power which comes with prayer will eventually win through.[3]

Never underestimate the righteous influence parents can have on their children. We never know when something some-

199

one says or does will touch them. All it takes is one spiritual experience to change a person's life. It is up to us, as parents, to create an environment where such experiences regularly take place. Under these conditions the windows of heaven will be opened, and the blessings of the Lord will be poured out. Such blessings are worth working for.

RESOURCES
TO HELP TEACH
THE GOSPEL
IN THE HOME

24

Brothers and Sisters as Resources

The way my eight-year-old son's head popped up reminded me of a puppet on a string. "Dad, I thought God, Jesus, and the Holy Ghost were three separate people."

"That's true. They are three separate, distinct beings."

"Then why did Jesus say they were all one person?"

We were reading our nightly chapter in the Book of Mormon. Adam, our sixteen-year-old, had just read 3 Nephi 11:27: "For behold, verily I say unto you, that the Father, and the Son, and the Holy Ghost are one; and I am in the Father, and the Father in me, and the Father and I are one."

Jimmy, our eight-year-old, had looked like he was half-asleep. However, he was paying much closer attention than I had thought. Susan, his twelve-year-old sister, had also picked up the apparent inconsistency.

With profound insight I began to explain this important gospel concept to my children, but Sam, our eighteen-year-old son, interrupted me. "Dad, may I try to explain it to them?"

"Sure, Son, go ahead."

Sam then clearly explained what the scripture meant, why it was written as it was, and how it applied to each of their lives. Frankly, I was very impressed. He did it much more simply than I would have, but what he said was consistent with gospel principles and indicated that he knew what he was talking about. Jimmy and Susan understood the explanation, so we continued reading.

After family prayer, Sam took me aside and said, "Dad, I apologize for interrupting you like that. I hope I didn't offend you. But I was concerned. You see, when you first explained that scripture to me, you fouled it up so badly that it took me months to figure it out. I didn't want that to happen to them."

After I thought about it for a minute, I realized he was probably right. I sometimes make simple things far too complex. But my greatest insight of the evening was a realization that my children can do a much better job of teaching each other the gospel than I had ever supposed.

Brothers and Sisters as Resources

When parents and children work and worship together, all the resources of the family come into play, and they are able to harness spiritual power available no other way. Under such circumstances, siblings have a profound influence on one another. Since children learn by example, the behavior of older brothers and sisters who keep the commandments becomes a testimony of the truthfulness of the principles their parents teach. Family norms are established, and the lessons of obedience, faith, charity, and integrity are reinforced. As a father of six boys explained, "One of the main reasons our five youngest sons served missions is because their oldest brother went and had such a great experience. The same is true for church attendance and the Word of Wisdom. When the older children live the gospel, our job as parents is much easier. When the younger children see the blessings that come from obedience, they are much more inclined to believe what we tell them."

Older children can contribute to teaching the gospel to their younger brothers and sisters in a variety of different ways. They can explain scriptures, advise against wrongdoing, share uplifting experiences, and warn against potential dangers and pitfalls. Indeed, one of the great benefits of reading the scriptures together as a family and holding regular family home evening is the opportunities children have to teach each other the gospel. Sometimes, however, they learn more through informal discussions. Note the comments from a stake president:

While growing up, I learned more about the gospel from

204

what was discussed at the dinner table than from any other single place. Dad and Mom told us stories from the scriptures and shared their own spiritual experiences. They also asked questions and directed discussions. We, as children, did the same. It was a comfortable setting (mainly because we liked to eat), and the environment was safe and conducive to learning. We were also a captive audience. Even though that happened over fifty years ago, I can clearly remember many of the discussions. They are wonderful memories.

These dinner table discussions can take a variety of formats. For example, in one family Sunday dinner is accompanied by a discussion of what each child learned in his or her classes that day. The father of three boys and a girl described his family's experiences in the following way:

> Each Sunday I ask the children what their teachers talked about that day. This process has several benefits. First, the children enjoy it, so it gives us something fun to talk about. Second, since they know they will be asked to share what they learned with the rest of the family, the children pay closer attention to their teachers. Third, the questions provide an excuse for us to informally discuss gospel principles. Fourth, if questions arise, we encourage the older children to teach the younger ones, which provides opportunities for them to bear their testimonies. And finally, it gives us a chance to correct doctrinal misunderstandings.
>
> For example, just as dessert was being served one Sunday, our seven-year-old boy said, "Dad, you forgot to ask us what we learned today."
>
> I said, "Hey, partner, you're right. What did your Primary teacher talk about today?"
>
> With a great deal of enthusiasm and excitement, he reported the following: "We talked about the plan of salvation. We start out in the pre-earth life, where we are all children of Heavenly Father. Then we come to earth, and the veil is pulled over us so we can't remember what it was like. Then we die, and we go to paradise if we lived right on earth. If we lived wrong, we go to prison. Then we have

205

the final judgment, and we go to the telestial kingdom if we have lived really bad. We go to the terrestrial kingdom if we are honest but don't join the Church. If we are baptized and keep all of Heavenly Father's commandments, we go to the *cholesterol* kingdom."

Children strongly influence the values of one another, and they can sometimes be more effective in teaching their siblings than their parents. Note the following example shared by a resourceful mother:

> I wanted to teach my five-year-old son the original twelve apostles in order, so that he would recognize them when we talked about them in family home evening and when we read the scriptures. However, after working with him for over an hour, I was getting nowhere. So I took his eight-year-old sister aside and asked her if she could teach him what I had failed to do. She smiled and said that she thought she could. The two of them then went into the living room and started to talk softly.
>
> Six minutes later, they came into the kitchen, smiling. Our daughter said she had an announcement to make. The task had been completed. Her brother then proudly recited the twelve apostles, in order of seniority, without missing a beat.

Because children have such a powerful influence on their brothers and sisters, they can also be a source of strength in times of difficulty. Consider the following example, related to us by the mother of seven children:

> When our son was eleven, he developed a serious problem with a lack of self-esteem. Kids at school were giving him a rough time; and as the fall progressed, he began to believe what they said and to really think of himself as a "nobody." As hard as we tried, we could not change that new and undesirable self-perception.
>
> Our fifteen-year-old daughter saw what was happening. As a secret Christmas present that year, she told us that she was going to give him a new self-image. With gentle tenacity she began her task. She consistently reminded him

206

of his positive attributes. She told him how cute she thought he was. She reinforced the things he did well and discounted his mistakes. She invited him to do things with her, and she bragged about him to her friends – often within listening distance of her brother.

We soon saw a miracle take place before our eyes. As a result of the love, the concern, and the caring that she manifested, he began to change. Within a year he honestly believed that he was as good as she had been telling him he was. He has since successfully fulfilled a mission, married in the temple, graduated from college, and now owns his own business. His success is directly related to his self-image; and that self-image is, to a great extent, a result of the care and concern shown by his older sister.

The counsel of an older brother or sister can also be a powerful force in changing undesirable behavior, as the following example illustrates:

Six weeks after school started, we learned that Doug, our third grader, was misbehaving in his choral music class. In fact, he prided himself on how much noise he could make and how disruptive he could be. I talked with him about it, and he promised me that he would stop. During the next two weeks, however, things only got worse.

I asked Judy, my twelve-year-old daughter, to talk with him. She agreed, as long as she could do it her way. That night, at the dinner table, Judy matter-of-factly said, "Doug, if I were you, I would be quiet in music class. If you don't, the teacher won't respect you, and the children will start to make fun of you."

Doug stopped chewing and quietly looked at his sister, who casually continued eating her salad. Nothing more was said about the subject.

One week later his music teacher called and asked, "What happened to Doug? That little kid has behaved like a jewel this past week. Whatever you're doing, keep it up."

A few days later, while sitting with Doug in the living room, I asked what made the difference. "Judy told me that the other kids and the teachers wouldn't like me. She's

207

already gone through grade school, and she had lots of friends. I just figured she knew what she was talking about, so I did what she said."

Obviously all problems cannot be resolved this easily. We certainly don't want to suggest that if older brothers and sisters merely talk with younger ones, all family problems will go away, because that won't happen. However, parents sometimes overlook their most obvious resources. Thus, our point is that siblings can be valuable resources to parents in teaching gospel principles, and wise parents will take advantage of all their resources in creating opportunities for children to have experiences with success.

25

The Role of
Grandparents

"I could tell something was out there by the way the sheep were acting. Some of the farmers had reported seeing a mountain lion in the area, and a few had even had some of their livestock killed. Generally, mountain lions don't attack humans, so I wasn't too worried about my own safety. Besides, before I left home that morning we knelt in family prayer, and my father asked the Lord to protect me from harm and danger. But the last thing I wanted that night was to have some of the sheep killed."

The eyes of my four children got as big as saucers. They had sat spellbound for over an hour as they listened to their grandfather tell stories about his life as a boy. I was fascinated by how effectively he wove gospel principles into the experiences he shared.

"But something was out there, all right. The sheep could always tell when a predatory animal was around. So I went out to see what was going on. All of a sudden, I saw it, and I froze in my tracks: a big mountain lion over by some rocks about fifty yards away. It scared me to death.

"Now I knew that animals are afraid of fire. So I immediately put more wood on the bonfire I had built earlier, including a long limb that had the end covered with sap, because I knew it would burn very quickly. All the while the dogs kept the lion away from the sheep as much as they could.

"But then the mountain lion snarled and started to come toward me. In order to protect myself, I grabbed the large limb from the fire and ran toward the lion, hoping to scare it away.

As I charged, the lion opened its mouth and snarled, so I stuck the burning limb right inside the lion's mouth. Thus the lion was persuaded to leave, and the sheep were protected." My children shrieked with mirth.

Dad then pointed his index finger at them and said, "Never underestimate the power of family prayer. Never. It is only because of the Lord's protection that I was not killed that night."

The Role of Grandparents

Grandparents can be extremely influential in helping their grandchildren understand the gospel and live Christlike lives. Indeed, the concepts discussed in this book apply as much to grandparents as to parents; and grandparents, in many instances, can reach children in ways that nobody else is able to do. In recalling a great teaching moment, a young elder said:

Dad traveled a lot when I was younger, so he wasn't around much to discipline us. When I turned thirteen, I started to talk back to my mother. One day, while visiting my grandparents, my grandmother talked with me privately. She told me about the importance of honoring my parents and asked me to be more respectful. Because of my love for that great woman, I promised to change my behavior. There are few people that I would have done that for.

Grandparents can also help their family members build links to their ancestors and gain a better understanding of their spiritual heritage. For example, the oldest of six children related the following experience about her grandmother:

Some of my most enjoyable childhood memories are the hours I spent at my grandmother's knee, listening to her talk about her own childhood and the lives of family members. Her mother walked across the plains when she was six. She watched the seagulls save the crops in the Salt Lake Valley. She attended the dedication of the Salt Lake Temple. Church history became much more meaningful for me once I realized that my great-grandmother was there when it happened.

Grandparents often have wonderful opportunities to render service to family members, particularly during times of serious illness and hardship. Such experiences often make indelible impressions on children. Note, for example, the experience of one grandson:

When I was six, my mom spent five weeks in the hospital. On several occasions she was so close to death that the doctors told my dad to notify the family. When they finally brought her home, my grandmother, who lived in our little town, spent weeks at our home. Even though that happened fifty years ago, I can still remember the rice puddings she fixed, the stories she read to me from the Bible, and the Primary songs we sang together.

Sometimes, because of family circumstances, grandparents have unusual opportunities to serve, as in the following example: "Since my mother always worked, many of my values came from my grandmother. She lived two doors from us and looked after me and my brother and sister; in fact, she raised us. My parents married outside the temple when they were very young, and they were never active in the Church. It is because of my grandmother that I am active in the Church today."

Because of their central role in the lives of family members, grandparents have unique opportunities to teach their grandchildren gospel principles.

I learned to serve others by watching my grandmother. She baked bread twice a week and always took a loaf to someone who needed it. I went with her on almost every delivery. She always canned an extra bushel of vegetables or fruit and took it to someone in need. It was just a way of life for her. She never wavered from it. Nobody ever asked her for help. She saw people in need and administered relief.

Children can also learn the meaning of gospel service from watching their grandparents.

I learned to love visiting teaching because Grandma enjoyed it so much. In fact, she loved to go visiting teaching.

211

She saw every one of her sisters every month. I never heard her complain about it. It was never a burden to her. She looked forward to going, and by doing so she instilled in me at a very young age a testimony of the importance of visiting teaching and the joy that comes from serving others.

However, not all children are fortunate enough to have grandparents who live close by. Nonetheless, grandparents can still positively influence their children. Letters from grandparents are highlights in a child's life, and they can make contributions to the lives of their posterity for generations to come. A mother of six shared the following experience:

> On the day my first child was born, my father wrote him a one-page letter in which he bore his testimony and expressed his love for me, for my husband, and for my new little boy. He also sent a little bank with three compartments — tithing, savings, and spending — and a silver dollar to start his missionary fund. He wrote, "I'm giving you this silver dollar in hopes that you will share the great blessings that you have received with others. My testimony and the first dollar of your missionary fund is an indication of the commitment of this family to serving the Lord and keeping his commandments." Dad has done this for each of his seventeen grandchildren. In the process, he has provided us with evidence of his love for the Lord and of the strength of his testimony.

Grandparents can also contribute to family unity in spite of distance. For example, a couple with seven children and twenty grandchildren started a family newsletter. The father described its impact on the lives of his grownup children and their children:

> After our seven children got married and moved away, they began to complain that they were losing touch with each other. Since they're scattered all over the world, communication is difficult and expensive. So we started a monthly newsletter. Each month they send us a two-page letter describing what has gone on in their families that month. We encourage them to also send pictures, graduation and ordination certificates, letters containing mission calls, awards, and anything else they think is important.

My wife and I assemble the material, make the copies, and send the packet to each family. The project takes us no more than two days a month, and it's really turned out to be a nice little project. The newsletter is a great way to keep in touch, since it brings everyone up to date on all the news. They put the packets in three-ringed binders, and the letters become a family history. We're essentially writing our family history a month at a time. It's painless, and it has done a great deal to strengthen our family ties.

Even if visits are limited to once a year or once every several years, private time with each child can have a lasting impact on a child's values. In one family, for example, the nonmember grandfather interviewed each of his grandchildren when they visited. Years later, his granddaughter reported the following:

> Some of my fondest childhood memories revolve around the private interviews my grandpa and I had. It was in that setting that I learned to love him and appreciate him for who he was. I knew that he loved me. I knew that I was important to him. I knew that he trusted me and really believed that I could be successful. Even though he wasn't a member of our church, he counseled me to keep the commandments, to be honest, and to be dependable. He sometimes said, "No, you don't want to do that," when I told him about something I was going to do. I also loved it when he said, "I'm darn proud of you." When I heard that, I wanted to do things that would make him even more proud of me.

Teaching does not have to be serious in order to be effective. A young missionary recently shared the following about his grandfather: "While driving along a sparsely traveled road with two of my cousins and me, Grandpa drove right down the middle of the road. He then looked at us and said, 'After I am dead and gone, and people ask you about your grandfather, you can tell them that he veered neither to the right nor to the left, and that he drove down the center of the road.' "

Grandparents can teach children unselfishness in a variety of different ways. Consider, for example, this grandfather's de-

213

scription of the unique way he and his wife teach their children and grandchildren to serve:

All of our children are married and rearing their own families. Some of them are really struggling, so they tend to get rather self-centered and forget that there are other people in the world who are worse off than they. Just before Thanksgiving each year we send each family two fifty-dollar bills, with the instructions that they can't spend one of them until they have spent the other on somebody less fortunate. It's amazing how creative they have become in serving others. It's also rewarding to see the joy that has come into their lives by forgetting about themselves and doing something for someone less fortunate.

Grandparents can also teach the gospel very effectively by their example, as the following illustrates:

I will never forget the few minutes I spent with my grandmother that winter evening. My wife and I were preparing to drive back to our home in Provo after visiting my grandmother in northern Utah. Thick fog had settled in, making driving hazardous. Before we left, my grandmother said, "Let's go in the other room and have prayer." We then knelt by the rocking chair in her living room, and I have never heard a person speak with the Lord so intimately, as if he were actually there, as did my grandmother that evening. I will never forget that experience. That happened almost thirty years ago, and I still can't describe that experience to others without weeping.

Consider as well the wonderful example this grandmother is setting for her posterity, as told by her granddaughter:

My eighty-four-year-old grandmother is the perfect example of how to address the problems of life. During the last eighteen months, her husband, her only remaining brother, and twelve of her close friends have died, and she has had two major operations. However, she continuously tells her children, "I have control over my life, and I refuse to let it get me down." To keep herself active, she daily reads the scriptures and other church books, and she rides her stationary bicycle several miles every day. She goes to the temple once each week, regularly visits the sick and less fortunate; and she never misses a baptism, a confirmation, an ordination, or a piano recital of her grand- and great-grandchildren. In spite of it all, she consistently prays that the Lord will help her to understand and fulfill her mission here in mortality.

Few people have the potential to play a more important role in the lives of children than their grandparents. They are great resources who can be relied upon to bless the lives of their posterity and instill righteous principles in the hearts and minds of family members.

26

You Don't Have to Do It Alone: Church Members and Friends as Resources

I could "smell" another one coming, just by the way he was talking. School had started three weeks earlier, and Brad, our six-year-old, loved his new teacher. As a result, much of his conversation around the dinner table centered on her. This particular evening he said, "She's really rich. In fact, I saw her paycheck today. She makes about ah, er, ah, ten million dollars a year!"

This was only one of a series of whoppers Brad had told in the past six weeks. They weren't malicious, in the sense that he wasn't telling lies about other people or trying to cover his own disobedience. They were just extreme exaggerations. But it was still dishonest. Furthermore, if this behavior continued, we would have some real problems. I had tried everything I knew to help him stop, but nothing worked.

During my interview with Frank Dixon, our home teacher, I mentioned the problem. Frank agreed to talk with Brad. So after his next visit to our home, he and Brad talked privately for a few minutes. At the end of their conversation, Brad promised to stop telling lies. The two of them also agreed that Frank would check with him periodically to see how he was doing.

To our home teacher, however, "periodically" meant every time Frank saw him: in the foyer before and after church services, during home-teaching visits, in the grocery store, and at the movie theater. Within three weeks the problem was resolved. With our home teacher's help, we were able to accomplish something my wife and I had been unable to do in twice the amount of time.

You Don't Have to Do It All by Yourself

For some parents the responsibility of teaching their children the gospel seems overwhelming. It's one thing to teach them gospel principles, but it's quite another to teach them in a way that they will learn. Although the responsibility for teaching our children the gospel falls on us as their parents, fortunately we don't have to do it alone. The Lord has provided others to help carry the burden. This includes home teachers, visiting teachers, other Church leaders, and friends.

Home Teachers and Visiting Teachers

The purpose of the Church and all its organizations and programs is to create eternal family units. To accomplish this, the Lord declared that those ordained to the priesthood have the responsibility to "teach, expound, exhort, baptize, and watch over the church . . . and visit the house of each member, exhorting them to pray vocally and in secret and attend to all family duties; . . . to watch over the church always, and be with and strengthen them; and see that there is no iniquity in the church, neither hardness with each other, neither lying, backbiting, nor evil speaking." (D&C 20:42-54.)

To fulfill this responsibility, the Church calls priesthood holders as *home teachers* to visit the homes of all Church members every month. They go in pairs, two Melchizedek Priesthood bearers as partners or one Aaronic Priesthood bearer accompanying a Melchizedek Priesthood bearer.

Effective home teaching can make a significant contribution to the lives of people. Since home teachers are called to work directly with families, they are in a better position to help the members of those families than are other Church officers or teachers. Thus, they should be the first people called in times of need.

For home teachers to be effective, however, family members must understand that their visitors are servants of the Lord and treat them accordingly. Sometimes that happens. Sometimes it doesn't, as the following example illustrates:

When I was fourteen, Dad and I were assigned to home

217

teach an inactive family who had gone through several sets of home teachers during the thirteen months since they moved into our ward. During our first visit we understood why. Five minutes after we arrived, their three little boys were making so much noise in the kitchen that we could hardly hear the TV, which remained on during our visit. After putting up with as much as she could stand, the mother yelled, "If you kids don't stop that noise, I'm going to make you come in here and listen to the home teachers!" They didn't make a sound for the rest of our visit. We were not surprised, therefore, that we had little impact on that family.

Instead, for home teachers to effectively bless families, we as parents need to support them and teach our children that they are the Lord's servants. A returned missionary described his experience as follows:

> I knew our home teachers were special because of the way my folks treated them. Whenever they came to our home, we stopped what we were doing and joined them in the living room. Before they left we always knelt in prayer and thanked the Lord for their visits. Whenever we had problems, our home teachers were the first people we called. Every time we knelt in family prayer, we prayed for them. As a result, when I was growing up, I thought our home teachers were the most important people in the Church!

Thus it should be in every home. Under such conditions, home teachers can be instruments in the Lord's hands in meeting the temporal and spiritual needs of family members.

When home teachers have clearly defined goals, they are better able to meet the family's needs. One of the easiest ways for parents to insure that effective home teaching takes place is for the head of the home to conduct regular interviews with his or her home teacher to identify needs and request help in specific areas. A single mother of three girls and a boy gave this account:

> By the time Steve was seven, I had no idea how to help him. There were things I simply couldn't do for him, like

218

fixing his bicycle and participating in sports activities. I also couldn't provide the adult male companionship that he so desperately needed.

I met with Brother Callister, our new home teacher, and explained my problem. A plan was put in place, and things started to happen. Once each week he and his son took Steve with them to the playground to play baseball, followed by a trip to the ice cream parlor. A bond of love developed, and Steve realized that he had a friend whom he could trust.

Brother Callister also went to work on building self-esteem in my son, which included helping with school work, giving positive feedback on things well done (and also on things not so well done), and teaching gospel principles during his monthly visits—all the while telling Steve what a great kid he was. When Steve turned eight, he and Brother Callister entered the baptismal font together.

Nobody can replace a young man's father. But Brother Callister has come as close as anyone possibly could. For the past six years, he has helped Steve build his pinewood derby cars, taken him on Scouting trips and family vacations, helped him repair his bicycle, encouraged him to start playing the trumpet, attended his concerts, assisted him in earning his Scouting ranks and badges, and created within him a burning desire to serve a mission. Steve considers Brother Callister his best friend and will do anything he suggests. Such is the power of an effective home teacher.

Visiting teachers can also provide wonderful assistance to families by delivering compassionate service and by helping mothers understand and fulfill their responsibilities. They make invaluable contributions to homes by teaching, inspiring, helping, and loving those whom they serve. A recently divorced mother of three young children described the help she has received:

> One of my visiting teachers has children about the same ages as mine. The other sister's children are much older. Both women have been extremely helpful to me as I face the challenge of rearing my children in the gospel. They

have become my closest and most trusted friends. Whenever I have problems, questions, or concerns about my children, I go to them for counsel. They bolster my confidence and share suggestions and ideas that have worked for them in rearing their own children. I know that I can call on them day or night for help, and they will respond. I no longer feel like I am alone. I thank my Heavenly Father daily for two visiting teachers who are consistently there when I need them.

Church Leaders

Church leaders are also valuable resources to parents in helping children learn and live the gospel. Priesthood and auxiliary leaders, teachers, and other Church officers can have a profound impact on the lives of young people. When leaders have consistent contact with our children, their influence can be far-reaching. Such was the case of a young man. Years later he described his experience this way.

> During the summer after my high-school graduation, I began dating a girl whose behavior was not consistent with gospel standards. I liked her a lot, and I could feel myself getting involved. On my way to Sunday School class one Sunday, I stopped to talk with the second counselor in the bishopric. For the next forty minutes we visited about college, missions, and marriage. Even though he was completely unaware of the dilemma I faced, his comments couldn't have been more to the point. He told me about his courtship with his wife and described the many blessings that had come into his life as a result of his marriage in the temple. As he spoke, the Spirit bore witness to me that the road I was on would not lead me where I wanted to go. I resolved at that moment to do nothing that would prevent me from serving a worthy mission and getting married in the temple. I will be forever grateful for that forty-minute conversation.

Church leaders can offer help and encouragement in areas that parents may not be able to do much in or supplement what parents are already doing. One father reported this fortunate experience that his fifteen-year-old daughter had:

220

Our Young Women's president was a dynamo, and the girls all loved her. But then she was released, and a talented but stricter leader was called. My daughter Lori was especially disappointed, and since she is quite talkative and independent, she and the new leader clashed a bit. My wife and I encouraged Lori to give the new leader time and pointed out that everyone has different styles of leadership.

The new president, because of her skills at dance, music, and art, expanded the range of the Young Women activities, and Lori at last found an outlet for her interest in song and dance. The leader helped coach her in learning a few songs for performance and let her practice on her piano. They have become close friends, and the leader has provided some opportunities for our daughter that my wife and I could not give her.

Friends

Good friends are of inestimable value. Interest in and subsequent activity in the Church for both members and nonmembers often result from close friendships. In fact, for many, their spiritual survival depends on the quality of those friendships. Therefore, we need to teach our children how to be good friends and how to develop close friendships with others. We also need to do all in our power to foster close friendships between our children and others with whom they share similar values. Obviously, we can't force children to like each other. But we can actively promote conditions under which those friendships can grow. The mother of five children described how her family handled this challenge:

> Bill was the only other deacon in our ward when we arrived here seventeen years ago. My husband and I realized that if Mike, our twelve-year-old, was to have any member friends, his choice was limited to one person. The two boys initially liked each other, so we had something positive to work with.
>
> Since the chances of them becoming good friends was hampered because they went to different junior high schools, we informally adopted Bill into our family and did

221

everything we could to foster that friendship. We invited him to Church activities and sleepovers on weekends. He spent most Sunday afternoons in our home. We used every excuse we could think of to get the two together for positive interaction. As a result, their friendship grew to the point that they became almost inseparable, and that friendship continued throughout high school. The strength they provided one another both protected them from difficulties and encouraged them during challenging times. Even though they have both returned from their missions, married in the temple, and have families of their own, they still remain in close contact.

In addition, close friendships for our children are not limited to children their own age. Adults can play key roles in the lives of children and can exercise a positive influence, teaching them to walk in the ways of the Lord. A father described the impact one elderly man has had on his ward and his own daughter:

> Earl Hammond is a saintly man whose life epitomizes humble and Christlike service to others. For over four decades he has blessed the lives of the members of the Boulder First Ward in the Boulder Colorado Stake. At age ninety (born in 1901), he is still the first to volunteer for welfare projects and temple assignments and to help new families moving into the area. Children flock to his side each Sunday to shake his hand and receive a warm greeting; he calls them all by name.
>
> Several years ago my seven-year-old daughter complained because she never got to see President Spencer W. Kimball. She asked, "Daddy, do you think President Kimball will ever come to our ward?"
>
> I responded, "There are so many wards in the Church and so many people who need him that he may never be able to visit our ward, sweetheart."
>
> She looked very contemplative. Then she smiled and with a great deal of excitement said, "Oh, that's okay. We don't need President Kimball. We have Brother Hammond!"

Parents need not feel that good influences are hard to find

outside the home. The more our children associate with good people, the greater their tendency to acquire characteristics and values consistent with gospel standards. Our children can be greatly blessed when we foster positive relationships between them and their home teachers, their Church leaders and friends, and the Brother Hammonds of the world.

27

Other Resources
to Help Lighten
the Load

The thought of it alone was enough to scare me to death. I had been a member of the Church for only six months, and I didn't even understand the gospel myself. How was I supposed to teach my children?

My role as single parent didn't help things either. My husband had died three years earlier, leaving me with three small children and few resources. When the missionaries taught us the first lesson seven months earlier, I immediately knew their message was true. My oldest daughter and I were baptized four weeks later.

When I shared my concern with my home teacher, he suggested that we might find something in the ward meetinghouse library that could give me some ideas. I was so naive that I didn't even know that the library existed! He made an appointment for the two of us the following evening.

As soon as we arrived, the librarian took us on a brief tour. I was amazed at the variety of resources available to Church members: filmstrips, videotapes, audiotapes, books, Church magazines, pictures, flannel boards, and lesson manuals. I was even more surprised to learn that members could check them out for use in their own homes. I had an entire library at my disposal, all at no cost!

The librarian handed me the Five Year Index to Periodicals of The Church of Jesus Christ of Latter-day Saints, January 1, 1981, to December 31, 1985. *She said that a new index came out every year, and every five years, the five yearly indexes were compiled into one large index. To my surprise, that one volume contained fifty-six references on the subject of teaching children. The three volumes for 1986–88 contained twenty-nine more. I had discovered a gold mine! Thirty minutes later I walked out of the library with a stack of publications containing nine articles on ways to help me more effectively teach the gospel to my children.*

Resources for Teaching the Gospel in the Home

Because of the magnitude of parents' responsibility to rear their children in light and truth, the task may, at first, seem overwhelming. Fortunately, parents are not left to themselves. Numerous resources exist to assist us in fulfilling this sacred responsibility. Examples include videocassettes, audiocassettes, music, and community resources.

Videocassettes

Videocassette technology provides a vehicle for gospel instruction that was impossible only a few years ago. Videotapes of general conference, Church broadcasts, and movies can aid parents in more effectively and memorably teaching children gospel principles. As a mother of six children explained:

> When I want to teach my children about the missions of John the Baptist and Peter, James, and John, we watch *The Restoration of the Priesthood. Johnny Lingo* portrays the destructive impact of criticism and the importance of self-esteem. *John Baker's Last Race* is a tear-jerker that contains important lessons about service and enduring to the end. And I don't know of a better way to help children understand the circumstances under which the Savior and Old Testament prophets taught the gospel than to watch *The New Media Bible: King James Version.*

> One advantage of using videotapes is the way they help children visualize what is going on. As my ten-year-old son said, "When I read the story about the restoration of the priesthood, I can see John the Baptist putting his hands on the heads of Joseph Smith and Oliver Cowdery. I can also see them standing in the river, with water running down their faces, hugging each other after they got baptized."

225

Videotapes also preserve important moments in Church history, such as general conference speeches. Fortunately, the conference talks are published and readily available. The printed word can provide a moving testimony to the reader. The visual presentation of the word, however, can provide added impact for children, as a father explained:

> During a recent family home evening, we had a lesson on the importance of developing a personal testimony. I will never forget the reaction of my three teenage children when they watched the tape of Elder Bruce R. McConkie sharing his final testimony in the April 1985 Annual General Conference, just ten days before his death. He said, "And now, as pertaining to this perfect atonement, wrought by the shedding of the blood of God — I testify that it took place in Gethsemane and at Golgotha, and as pertaining to Jesus Christ, I testify that he is the son of the Living God and was crucified for the sins of the world. He is our Lord, our God, and our King.
>
> "I am one of his witnesses, and in a coming day I shall feel the nail marks in his hands and in his feet and shall wet his feet with my tears.
>
> "But I shall not know any better then than I know now that he is God's Almighty Son, that he is our Savior and Redeemer, and that salvation comes in and through his atoning blood and in no other way."[1]
>
> As Elder McConkie's voice broke with emotion, I looked at my children. All three of them were weeping. After he finished his sermon, we sat in silence for several minutes. It was one of those unforgettable experiences that bless our lives.

Because of their effectiveness in teaching, the Church has made a major commitment to provide resources via videotapes, and the number of movies, speeches, and broadcasts in that format is growing rapidly.

Audiotapes

The abundance of material available on audiotape makes this an extremely valuable resource for teaching children; and the portability of these tapes makes their enjoyment possible under a variety of different circumstances. They also provide opportunities for gospel study that are both instructive and time-saving. One father, for example, reported that he had listened to the entire Book of Mormon during a three-week period while driving to and from work. A mother of five children had listened to *Jesus the Christ* three times in six months while running errands with her children.

Parents don't always know how much information their children actually absorb from these informal teaching experiences. Often, however, they pick up much more than we realize. As one father said:

> For several years I listened to tapes of the scriptures while driving my car. Whenever I ran errands, I always invited my children to accompany me. Since those errands frequently took us by the local ice-cream shop, the children gladly came along.
>
> Years later, when my oldest son started early morning seminary, he studied the New Testament. After a month of getting up at 5:30 A.M., he reported that he loved seminary and found that the exams were a snap. He said that from listening to the tapes while running errands with me as a youngster, he practically had the four Gospels memorized!

A mother whose family makes a semiannual eleven-hour trip from Colorado to Utah each year to visit relatives reported the advantage of using travel time to teach her children:

> Whenever we drive to Utah, we always listen to *Charlie's Monument* and *The Bishop's Horse Race*, two of Blaine and Brenton Yorgason's books that have been put on audiotape. They are fun. They contain important gospel messages for children; and they make the scenery through the desert stretches almost bearable.
>
> On the way back, we usually listen to tapes on the life of Christ. We start them as we leave Salt Lake City, and they typically finish about the time we arrive home. They make the time go more quickly; and they are great tools for teaching my children the gospel in ways that they enjoy.

Children's stories of the Old Testament, New Testament, Book of Mormon, and Church history are available on audiotape with companion books in a cartoon format, written at the second-grade level. As a result, children can learn the gospel in a medium that they love—cartoons. A young mother shared how she taught her daughter to love the scriptures:

> Every night before my four-year-old daughter goes to bed, I put on one of the tapes from either the *New Testament Stories* or *Book of Mormon Stories* and let her follow along in the cartoon book. She has the stories almost memorized, and I often hear her telling them to her two-year-old sister. She has developed a love for the scriptures and, when given a choice, prefers listening to stories from the scriptures to watching television.

The advantage of many of these tapes is that they are entertaining and, at the same time, deliver important gospel messages in ways with which children can identify. The more enjoyable that learning the gospel can be, the greater the tendency for chidren to believe what they hear. Even the weekly cleaning of a bedroom can be made enjoyable with the tape recorder on.

Music

Music is the universal language of feelings and emotions. Thus, few things have the capacity to edify, inspire, and touch our souls quite like good music. In the preface to the Church hymnbook, the First Presidency said:

> Music has boundless powers for moving families toward greater spirituality and devotion to the gospel. Latter-day Saints should fill their homes with the sound of worthy music. . . . The hymns can bring families a spirit of beauty and peace and can inspire love and unity among family members.
>
> Teach your children to love the hymns. Sing them on the Sabbath, in home evening, during scripture study, at prayer time. Sing as you work, as you play, and as you travel together. Sing hymns as lullabies to build faith and testimony in your young ones.[2]

The availability of Church hymns on audiocassette has made following this counsel possible for every family in the Church. For about the price of two commercially made audiotapes, members can buy all eighteen cassettes containing every hymn in our hymnbook. As a result, the opportunity for children to learn and enjoy the sacred hymns of the Restoration has increased manyfold. Note the comments of a mother of six children, three of whom are of preschool age:

> Little did I know at the time I bought them what a valuable resource it would be—for less than a dollar a tape. We play them continuously in our home and when we travel in the car. The younger children have many of them memorized and sing along enthusiastically whenever they are played. This single item has added a greater dimension of spirituality to our home than any single thing we have ever done.

A fifteen-year-old girl also described the impact that the hymns have on her: "Whenever I hear them, they remind me of special occasions when I have felt the Holy Ghost. 'Onward Christian Soldiers' reminds me of my brother's missionary farewell. When I hear 'I Believe in Christ,' I can see in my mind Elder Marvin J. Ashton sitting on the stand in our stake conference, and I remember how strongly I felt the Spirit. That was one of the most spiritual times of my life."

If we want our children to have spiritual experiences, we must invite the Spirit to come into our homes. One of the best ways to do that is to sing the hymns together. As one teenage girl explained:

> Singing hymns is an easy way to bring the Spirit into your life. Some are very reverent, while others are really fun to sing. Some of my fondest memories are of our family singing our favorite hymns as we stood around the piano. My little brother and I sang the melody, Dad sang bass, and Mom played. I'm sure people would have found it hilarious if they had heard us, but we still enjoyed it. Sometimes we even sounded pretty good!

In describing the benefit of hymns on us as individuals, the

First Presidency said, "Hymns can lift our spirits, give us courage, and move us to righteous action. They can fill our souls with heavenly thoughts and bring us a spirit of peace."[3] For example, note the experience of a fourteen-year-old girl after a particularly difficult day:

> It had been the worst day of my life. Everything had gone wrong. My friends got mad at me. I forgot some assignments. I flunked a test. And to top it off, I had a lousy soccer practice, and the coach yelled at me. I felt awful.
>
> When my dad and little brother picked me up from school, they had the hymns playing in the car. I immediately felt the Holy Ghost. It really hit the spot; and it's the only thing that I know of that could have helped me so much so quickly. As soon as I closed the door, I felt better. Within less than a block, I was singing along with them and thoroughly enjoying myself.

The Lord said, "For my soul delighteth in the song of the heart; yea, the song of the righteous is a prayer unto me." (D&C 25:12.) Thus music can also be a source of strength in times of physical difficulty and danger. Consider, for example, the experience of a soldier who served in Vietnam:

> One night, as my buddies and I returned from a mission, we had to cross an area infested with land mines. Many of my colleagues had lost their lives on similar assignments. I remember repeating, over and over, the words to the song I had learned as a child: "Lead me, guide me, walk beside me. Help me find the way." Indeed, that song became as sincere a prayer as I had ever offered.

Gospel-oriented music creates a spiritual atmosphere and sends messages in unmistakable terms as to what a family stands for and the kind of climate that is desired. As Lex De Azevedo explained, "When we consider music's impact on us, and how many thousands of hours we listen to it throughout our lives, it seems wise to choose for ourselves and our families music which builds up our spiritual reserves rather than that which continually wears them down."[4] As family members sing the hymns of the Restoration together, they build traditions and create spiritual experiences that, in turn, build testimonies and feelings of love that they will cherish for a lifetime.

Community Resources

The thirteenth Article of Faith affirms, "If there is anything virtuous, lovely, or of good report or praiseworthy, we seek after these things." Fortunately, most communities have a variety of activities and resources that can contribute to the richness of family members' lives.

For example, through public libraries, museums, art galleries, local music guilds, symphony orchestras, and drama, children can obtain materials and attend activities that will help them gain an appreciation for the beautiful, aesthetic things in life. Many of these materials and activities are free or available at little cost. Most cities, for instance, have numerous free concerts and recitals, readings, and art displays every year. Many libraries offer free story times, plays, and workshops (as well as tapes, movies, and posters that can be checked out).

A mother described her own experience the following way: "Each year during junior high and high school, I attended the community symphony concert series with my mother. As a result, I learned to love classical music, to the point that if given a choice, I preferred classical music to the popular music of the time. That love remains with me to this day."

As children come to appreciate and value things that are virtuous, lovely, of good report, and praiseworthy, they will be less inclined to participate in activities that are contrary to gospel standards.

Notes

PREFACE

1. Spencer W. Kimball, address given at the MIA June Conference Closing Session, June 23, 1974, 7.

CHAPTER 1

1. DeLynn Decker, " 'You Are a Marked Generation,' President Benson Tells Students," report of address given at the Southern California Student Devotional, Anaheim Convention Center Arena, 8 February 1987, *Ensign*, April 1987, 73.

2. For example, see Gen. 18:19; Deut. 6:5–7; 1 Sam. 3:13; Prov. 22:6; Eph. 6:4; 2 Ne. 4:3; Mosiah 4:14–15; Alma 35:16; Moses 6:41, 56–58; 8:27.

3. Ezra Taft Benson, "Great Things Required of Their Fathers," *Ensign*, May 1981, 34–35.

4. Marion G. Romney, "Home Teaching and Family Home Evening," *Improvement Era*, June 1969, 97.

5. Joseph F. Smith, *Conference Report*, April 1910, 6.

6. David O. McKay, "Seeds of Happiness in the Soul," *Instructor*, October 1960, 322.

CHAPTER 2

1. Joseph Fielding Smith, "Counsel to the Saints and to the World," *Ensign*, July 1972, 27; italics added.

2. David O. McKay, "Unity of Purpose Important to the Accomplishment of God's Work," *Improvement Era*, December 1967, 35.

3. David O. McKay, "Blessed Are They That Do His Commandments," *Improvement Era*, June 1964, 445.

CHAPTER 3

1. See Leland R. Nelson, comp., *Journal of Joseph: the Personal Diary of a Modern Prophet* (Provo, Utah: Council Press, 1979), 196.

NOTES

2. See Andrew F. Ehat and Lyndon W. Cook, eds., *Words of Joseph Smith* (Provo: Religious Studies Center, Brigham Young University, 1980), 37.

CHAPTER 4

1. Dallin H. Oaks, "Recognize Spirit When It Is Manifest," *Church News,* April 29, 1989, 14.

2. See Mosiah 4:3, 20; D&C 6:23; 11:13.

3. See John 14:16–18, 26.

4. See Neh. 9:20; John 15:26; 16:13; Moro. 10:5; D&C 136:32–33.

5. See Mosiah 4:2–3; D&C 76:118.

6. See Ps. 143:10; Eph. 5:9; D&C 11:12.

7. See Prov. 1:23; Joel 2:28.

CHAPTER 5

1. Brigham Young, *Journal of Discourses,* 14:192.

CHAPTER 6

1. Ezra Taft Benson, *To the Mothers in Zion,* pamphlet (Salt Lake City: The Church of Jesus Christ of Latter-day Saints, 1987), 8–9.

2. Benson, *To the Mothers,* 8–9.

3. Dale Carnegie, *How to Win Friends and Influence People,* rev. ed. (New York: Pocket Books, 1981), 15–17.

4. Ashley Montague, as quoted in A. Theodore Tuttle, "The Things That Matter Most," *Ensign,* December 1971, 90.

CHAPTER 7

1. Foster W. Cline, *Parent Education Text* (Evergreen, Colorado: Evergreen Consultants in Human Behavior, 1982), 77–78.

2. See Cline, 78–79.

CHAPTER 8

1. L. Tom Perry, "Train Up a Child," *Ensign,* May 1983, 77; italics added.

2. Marion G. Romney, "Let Us Set in Order Our Own Houses," *Ensign,* January 1985, 5.

3. Joseph Fielding Smith, *Conference Report,* October 1948, 153.

4. Joseph Fielding Smith, comp., *Teachings of the Prophet Joseph Smith* (Salt Lake City: Deseret Book Company, 1976), 328.

CHAPTER 9

1. David O. McKay, "Unity of Purpose," 34.

2. Boyd K. Packer, "Agency and Control," *Ensign,* May 1983, 66.

NOTES

3. Boyd K. Packer, "Revelation in a Changing World," *Ensign,* November 1989, 15.

4. Brigham Young, *Journal of Discourses,* 4:297–98.

5. David O. McKay, *Gospel Ideals* (Salt Lake City: Improvement Era, 1953), 143.

6. Gordon B. Hinckley, "Keeping the Temple Holy," *Ensign,* May 1990, 51.

7. Dallin H. Oaks, "Criticism," *Ensign,* February 1987, 68.

8. Oaks, "Criticism," 70.

9. Oaks, "Criticism," 70.

10. Gene W. Dalton, "Insight and Responsibility," *Commissioner's Lecture Series, 1974,* Church Educational System, 4.

CHAPTER 10

1. Jim Fay, *Tickets to Success* (Evergreen, Colorado: Cline/Fay Institute, Inc., 1988), 40.

CHAPTER 11

1. Francis M. Lyman, "Proprieties of Prayer," *Improvement Era,* April 1947, 245.

2. See Bruce R. McConkie, *Mormon Doctrine* (Salt Lake City: Bookcraft, 1958), 581–82.

3. Clare Middlemiss, ed., *Cherished Experiences from the Writings of President David O. McKay* (Salt Lake City: Deseret Book, 1976), 6–7.

4. Loren C. Dunn, "This Is My Beloved Son," *Ensign,* December 1971, 48.

5. Spencer W. Kimball, *The Teachings of Spencer W. Kimball,* ed. Edward L. Kimball (Salt Lake City: Bookcraft, 1982), 117.

CHAPTER 12

1. Ezra Taft Benson, "The Power of the Word," *Ensign,* May 1986, 79, 81.

2. Marion G. Romney, *Conference Report,* April 1960, 112–13.

3. Benson, "Power of the Word," 82.

4. Dennis and Sandra Packard, *Feasting upon the Word* (Salt Lake City: Bookcraft, 1981), ix-x.

5. Packard, 207–8.

6. J. Richard Clarke, "My Soul Delighteth in the Scriptures," *Ensign,* November 1982, 14.

CHAPTER 13

1. Spencer W. Kimball, *Faith Precedes the Miracle* (Salt Lake City: Deseret Book, 1972), 271; italics added.

NOTES

2. Kimball, *Teachings,* 137.

3. Kimball, *Teachings,* 211.

CHAPTER 14

1. First Presidency, "Editors' Table: Home Evening," *Improvement Era,* June 1915, 733–34.

2. Dallin H. Oaks, "Parental Leadership in the Family," *Ensign,* June 1985, 11.

3. Oaks, "Parental Leadership," 11.

4. Spencer W. Kimball, "Train Up a Child," *Ensign,* April 1978, 2.

CHAPTER 15

1. Kimball, *Teachings,* 250–51.

2. Boyd K. Packer, *That All May Be Edified* (Salt Lake City: Bookcraft, 1982), 12.

CHAPTER 16

1. See McConkie, *Mormon Doctrine,* 166–68.

2. Thomas S. Monson, *Favorite Quotations from the Collection of Thomas S. Monson* (Salt Lake City: Deseret Book Company, 1985), 61.

3. Lorenzo Snow, *Journal of Discourses,* 4:184.

4. Joseph F. Smith, "Sermon on the Home Government," *Liahona, The Elders' Journal,* October 1911, 260-61.

CHAPTER 17

1. See Kimball, *Teachings,* 349.

2. Wilford Woodruff, March 17, 1857, entry; in Scott G. Kenney, ed., *Wilford Woodruff's Journal, Volume 5, 1 January 1857–31 December 1861* (Midvale, Utah: Signature Books, 1984), 39; italics added.

3. Spencer W. Kimball, "The Angels May Quote from It," *New Era,* October 1975, 5.

4. For a helpful guide to creating family records, see Don Norton, *Composing Your Life Story: Ten Practical Guides to Creating a Personal History* (Orem, Utah: Don Norton, 1982).

CHAPTER 19

1. See Fay, *Tickets to Success,* 57–93.

CHAPTER 20

1. Joseph Harris, personal communication to authors, July 17, 1989.

CHAPTER 21

1. Fay, *Tickets to Success,* 29.

2. For additional information on family rules, see William G. Dyer and Phillip

236

R. Kunz, *Effective Mormon Families: How They See Themselves* (Salt Lake City: Deseret Book Company, 1986), 44–48.

3. See Fay, *Tickets to Success*, 81.

4. Jim Fay, *Helicopters, Drill Sergeants, and Consultants* (Evergreen: Cline/Fay Institute, Inc., 1988), 95–96.

5. Victor B. Cline, *How to Make Your Child a Winner* (New York: Walker & Company, 1980), 86.

CHAPTER 22

1. Blaine M. Yorgason, personal communication to authors, November 2, 1989.

CHAPTER 23

1. Joseph F. Smith, Jr., "Is Man Immortal?" *Improvement Era*, March 1916, 426.

2. Orson F. Whitney, *Conference Report*, April 1929, 110–11.

3. Gordon B. Hinckley, "The Environment of Our Homes," *Ensign*, June 1985, 3–4.

CHAPTER 27

1. Bruce R. McConkie, "The Purifying Power of Gethsemane," *Ensign*, May 1985, 11.

2. *Hymns of The Church of Jesus Christ of Latter-day Saints* (Salt Lake City: Deseret Book, 1985), x.

3. *Hymns*, x.

4. Lex De Azevedo, *Pop Music and Morality* (North Hollywood, California: Embryo Books, 1982), 115.

Index

239

importance of keeping covenants,
128–29; importance of being
supportive in, 129; elements of
successful, 129–32; samples of,
130–31, 133–38; enhancing self-
esteem through, 132; enforcing
decisions of, 133–38
Criticism, destructive nature of, 9,
37–38, 40–41, 63–66

Dalton, Gene, 65
De Azevedo, Lex, 230
Death of mother, examples
concerning, 28–29, 83–84
Decision making. *See* Choices;
Mistakes
Discipline and covenant interview,
124
Dixon, Frank, 216
Dunn, Loren C., 84–85

Earthquake, Samoan home protected
in, 175–76
Empathy, showing, 163, 184–85
Example, impact of, 29–33, 57, 115,
204

Faith, developing, 81–82
Family: participation of, in special
fast, 7–8; as most important
organization, 8; building unity in,
9–10, 12; holding problem-
solving meetings in, 12–13;
holding testimony meetings with,
26–27; prayers in, 84–86; rules in,
180–81. *See also* Home
Family home evening: making,
enjoyable, 55; youth feels blessed
because of, 106–7; introduction of
concept of, 107; resource book
for, 107–8; flexibility in, 108–9;
music in, 109; holding, regularly,
109–10; children's input in, 110–
11; blessings accompanying, 111–
13; keeping records in, 148–51;
allows siblings to help in gospel
teaching, 204

Fasting, 7–8, 13, 18
"Father Forgets," 39–41
Fault finding, 37–38, 40–41, 63–66
First Presidency statement on
hymns, 228
Forgiveness, setting example of, 32
Friendship: between parents and
children, 35–39, 41–43; criticism
ruins, with children, 40–41;
potential of, for righteous
influence, 221–23

God: developing relationship with,
through prayer, 81–82; words of,
are contained in scriptures, 87;
worship of, is purpose of church
meetings, 98–99
Good Neighbor Policy: applying, to
children, 46, 51; explanation of,
46–47; handling problems with,
47–51
Gospel: teaching, is parents'
responsibility, 3–6; and self-
esteem, 11; principles of, modeled
by parents, 29–33; instilling desire
to obey, 54–55, 57–58; teaching
principles of, through prayer, 80–
81; using vacations to teach, 152–
57; teaching, to missionaries, 187–
92; brothers and sisters can help
teach, 203–8; dinner-table
discussions of, 205–6;
grandparents as teachers of,
teachings, 209–10, 212–15;
grandparents as teachers of,
service, 211–13; publications to
help teach, 224–25; audiovisual
materials to help teach, 225–28;
music to help teach, 228–30
Gossip, teen solves problem of, 164–
69
Grandparents: experiences of,
teaching gospel through, 209–10,
214–15; powerful influence of,
210, 215; provide link to
ancestors, 210; service rendered

240

by, 211–12; long-distance, 212–13; teaching opportunities of, 213–14

Hammond, Earl, 222
Harris, Joseph, 176
Hinckley, Gordon B., 63, 198–99
Holy Ghost: helping children recognize, 17, 25, 27; having companionship of, 18; influence of, in righteous homes, 19–20; felt in Sunday School class, 21–22; testimony comes through, 22; failure to recognize witness of, 22–23; children have capacity to understand, 23–24; scriptures describe feelings associated with, 26; service invites presence of, 115–16; promptings of, to help others, 118–19. *See also* Spiritual experiences
Home: joys of, 5–6; love in, works miracles, 13; spiritual experiences in, 19–20. *See also* Family
Home teachers, help of, in teaching gospel, 216–19
Hymns, edifying influence of, 228–31

Interviews. *See* Covenant interview

Jesus Christ, love for, motivates service, 119–20
Journal: youth quotes from, in sacrament meeting talk, 140–41; recording spiritual experiences in, 142–44; encouraging children to keep, 144–45. *See also* Record keeping

Kimball, Spencer W.: on blessings of family prayer, 85; on worshipping God in meetings, 98; on commandments as program for happiness, 105; lists eight ingredients for successful family home evening, 108; on gospel teaching offsetting world's negatives, 112–13; on lifting others' burdens, 116; on keeping journals, 144

Lameco, Vialua, 175–76
Language, scriptural, familiarizing children with, 91
Larned, Livingston, 39–41
Lawn mower, broken, sample reactions to, 46–47
Leaders, Church: supporting, 60; "blind" obedience to, 60–63; mistakes made by, 61–62; dangers of criticizing, 63–66; helping children develop confidence in, 66–67; as resources for teaching gospel, 220–21
Letters to missionaries, 187–92
Library, ward, resources available in, 224–25
Listening, importance of, 131
Love, power of, 13, 132; of God, 81–82
Lunch, daughter joins mother for, 34–35
Lying, covenant interview helps son overcome, 136–38

McConkie, Bruce R., 226
McConkie, Mark, 96–97
McKay, David O.: on joys of home, 5–6; on focusing on positive, 9; on love in home, 13; on honoring and respecting priesthood, 60; on criticizing Church leaders, 63; on gaining testimony over time, 82–83; shares boyhood experience with sacrament prayer, 103–4
Meetings: children fuss about attending, 98, 193–94; purpose of sacrament, is to worship, 98–99; developing habit of attending, 99–100; irreplaceable experiences at, 100–105; speakers in sacrament, 114–15, 139–41, 152–53; sacrament, while on vacation, 154–55

Miracles promised to loving families, 13–14
Missionaries: letters to, 187, 189–92; teaching gospel to, 187–88
Mistakes: making it safe to admit, 49; of Church leaders, 61–62; learning from, 71, 179–80, 183; keeping price of, affordable, 71–73; inevitability of, 197
Monson, Thomas S., 123
Motivation, avoiding criticism in, 38
Music, using, 109, 228–31

Neighbors. *See* Good Neighbor Policy
"No" as answer to prayer, 83–84
Noah, days of, compared to today, 3

Oaks, Dallin H., 23, 63–65, 107–8
Obedience: spiritual experiences contingent upon, 52–53; importance of, 54; instilling desire for, 54–55, 57–58; tied to priesthood ordinances, 56–57; is not always convenient, 57; and personal revelation, 58; "blind," 60–63
Ordinances, priesthood: reverent treatment of, 31–32; preparing for, 56–57, 171–72; keeping records of, in journal, 142–43; boy helps friend understand, 170–71; discussing, in advance, 171–72; reinforcing importance of, 172–74, 177–78; responsibilities involved in accepting, 174–75; testifying of power of, 175–76

Packer, Boyd K., 61–62, 119
Patience, exercising, with wayward children, 198–99
Perry, L. Tom, 54
Personal histories, 147–48
Positives, focusing on, 9–10, 42
Power struggles. *See* Rebellion
Prayer: example of, set in family, 29; of girl whose family left her at church building, 79–80; public

and private, 80; teaching gospel principles through, 80–81; learning of children's problems through, 81; teaches love for Heavenly Father, 81–82; accepting "no" as answer to, 83–84; with families, 84–86; for help in resolving problems, 162–63
Premortality, character development in, 197
Priesthood: reverent treatment of ordinances of, 31–32; preparing to receive ordinances of, 56–57; supporting and honoring, 60; importance of, demonstrated by personal examples, 173–76. *See also* Ordinances, priesthood
Priorities, developing, in relationships, 38–39
Problem solving: family holds meetings for, 12–13; and Good Neighbor Policy, 47–51; in covenant interview, 126–27; role of prayer in, 162–63; five steps for helping children with, 163; illustration of process of, 164–69; help of siblings in, 206–8
Promises, written, in covenant interview, 135, 137

Quarreling, destructiveness of, 10

Rebellion: due to lack of choices, 74–76; preventing, through early teaching, 194; as power struggle, 194–95; gospel approach to dealing with, 195; identifying roots of, 195–96; refusing to be dragged down by, 196–97; maintaining patience despite, 198–99
Record keeping: importance of, 141, 151; in journals, 142–45; in scrapbooks, 145–46; of children's quotes, 146–47; in personal histories, 147–48; using audiotapes and videotapes in,

148; in family home evenings,
148–51
Responsibility: letting children
assume, for problems, 49–51, 163;
developed through making
mistakes, 71–73, 179–80, 183;
increases in, timed with
priesthood ordinances, 173–74;
sacred, involved in accepting
ordinances, 174–75; teaching,
involves pain, 180; role of rules
in, 180–81; role of chores in, 181–
83; teaching, by holding children
accountable, 183–85
Revelation, personal, 58, 63, 118–19;
questioning of, by antagonists,
61. *See also* Holy Ghost
Richards, George F., 64
Rigdon, Sidney, 4
Romney, Marion G., 5, 54, 88
Rules, importance of, in teaching
responsibility, 180–81

Sacrament: mother sets example of
reverence for, 31–32; David O.
McKay fumbles with prayer on,
103–4; mother impressed with
blessing on, 155; preparing to
offer blessing on, 172
Sacrament meetings. *See* Meetings
Samoa, earthquake in, home
protected from, 175–76
Satan, strengthening children against
tactics of, 5, 8–9
Scrapbooks, 145–46
Scriptures: insights in, on
recognizing Holy Ghost, 26;
importance of studying, 87–89;
gospel questions generated by,
90; reading, aloud, 91; schedule
and method of studying, 92–94;
focusing on stories in, 94–95;
using audiotapes of, 95–96, 227–
28; learning to love, 97; brother
explains, to younger siblings,
203–4
Self-esteem, 10–12, 132, 206–7

Service, importance and teaching of,
115–20, 211–12
Sheriff, teenage son's run-in with,
44–45
Smith, Joseph, 4, 18, 58, 162, 197–98
Smith, Joseph F., 5, 107, 12, 1973
Smith, Joseph Fielding, 8, 57–58
Snow, Lorenzo, 130
Spiritual experiences: creating climate
for, 18; do not happen by
accident, 18; keys to having, 19;
in righteous homes, 19–20;
having, without recognizing
them, 22–23; pointing out
instances of, 25; contingent upon
obedience, 52–53; associated with
family prayer, 85–86; at church
meetings, 99, 101, 102–5;
associated with service, 115–16,
118–19; shared in covenant
interviews, 132; keeping records
of, 141–43; on vacations, 152–57;
sharing, in letters to missionaries,
191; inviting, through uplifting
music, 229
Stake conference, attending, 100–101
Sunday, girl attends party on, 72–73

Temple, family and, 156, 177–78
Testimony, building, 22, 26–27, 82–
83, 99
Thanksgiving dinner, family shares,
17
Time, investment of, in developing
friendship with children, 42–43
Tithing, parents' example in paying,
30–31
Trust, importance of, 35–37, 126
Tuimaseve, Misiona, 176

Unity, developing, 9–13, 63, 86, 110

Vacations: teaching gospel during,
152–54, 156–57; attending
sacrament meetings while on,
154–55
Values, adopting, of parents, 30